Endorsements for Blueprints for Children's Ministry

Whether your children's ministry program is well developed, in need of tweaking, or just beginning, *Blueprints for Children's Ministry* is a great resource for envisioning, planning, and conducting a vibrant ministry for children. Kim E. Bestian guides readers through a step-by-step process useful in building a Children's Ministry program. Included are a wealth of blueprint samples of components that can be readily adapted to the ministry of your church. Her inspiration for Children's Ministry is hearing children express, "I can't wait to be there." This can be your inspiration too!

Rebecca S. Schmidt, Ed.D.
Associate Director of Schools, The Lutheran Church—Missouri Synod

When you read *Blueprints for Children's Ministry*, you will read the passion and love Kim has for children and her Lord and Savior. She has shared a comprehensive blueprint for any congregation to engage in a most important part of the church's mission: children's ministry! Kim's *Blueprints* is written so you can design for your congregation the scope and realm of what you plan to do and how to go there, with evaluations along the way. What a beautiful description to help and encourage congregations for the wonderful mission and ministry for children. Well done, Kim; the Lord bless your endeavors in sharing *Blueprints for Children's Ministry*!

Rev. Allen D. Anderson
President, Rocky Mountain District, and Pastor, Mount Zion Lutheran Church

Blueprints for Children's Ministry should be open on the desk of every congregational leader. Kim E. Bestian, an experienced Director of Children's Ministry with a huge heart for God's youngest ones, has put together a book that can help every church build its ministry for and with children from the ground up. Biblically based in every aspect, *Blueprints* is easy to read and follow. This book not only shows the reasons for a good children's ministry program, but it also takes congregations step by step through the whole process, including a set of "blueprints" that ensures every phase along the way.

Martha Streufert Jander
Author, Editor, and Early Childhood Consultant

I am thrilled that Kim Bestian has reflected upon her years of children's ministry to share insights in this ready-to-go volume helping churches and schools nurture faith in children from birth through grade 6. Prepared blueprints offer examples to accomplish each task. Whether you are beginning a children's ministry or want to expand or evaluate an existing program, *Blueprints for Children's Ministry* will guide you through the process. Focusing on important elements of children's ministry, such as Christian education, ministry opportunities for children, and parental relationships, Kim coaches readers to build a program and prepare a team to accomplish your goals.

Laurie A. Friedrich, Ph.D.
Teaching, Learning, & Teacher Education, University of Nebraska-Lincoln

D1567072

Thank God for equipping Kim Bestian to speak on behalf of children and the church's ministry to them and their families! *Blueprints* is a perfect name for this resource chock-full of attractive, user-friendly, ready-to-use, practical samples. These reproducible pages provide leaders with tools to lay a solid foundation, build a sound ministry, and creatively grow their attempts to reach more children for Jesus—children who will exclaim, "I can't wait to be there!"

Cynthia Brown, Ph.D.
Adjunct Professor, Family Life, Concordia University, Ann Arbor,
and author, *Energizing Your Children's Ministry*

The analogy of using a construction framework to building a children's ministry is a concrete (no pun intended) approach to explaining the necessary blueprints needed for anyone seeking to launch or restructure the children's ministry in their church. This extremely useful step-by-step resource focuses first and foremost on raising up young disciples and the impact the church has on nurturing their faith. You will learn practical information as it relates to volunteers, curriculum, safety, parent collaboration, and much more. The Scripture passages throughout remind us that God as the Foreman will be the one leading your children's ministry to fruition. From hard hats and safety glasses to the armor of God, you have the opportunity to stand firm and take up the shield of faith as you begin this exciting endeavor.

Melissa A. Smith
Assistant Professor and Early Childhood Coordinator,
College of Education, Concordia University Chicago

Blueprints for Children's Ministry is a relevant, needed, and timely resource. The state of our world makes it essential to teach children and disciple families so parents have models for sharing the faith with their children. From safety guidelines, peacemaking, discipline, and teacher training, this book contains great resources for getting started with children's ministry. It will let you avoid reinventing the wheel while creating a vibrant, Gospel-sharing, child ministry program.

Kim Marxhausen, Ph.D.
Education consultant, author, and speaker

Written from the heart, this book provides valuable insight into the importance of children's ministry in the Church, as well as the many directions in which such a ministry can go. Drawing on years of experience in children's ministry, the author includes many practical suggestions for establishing and maintaining such a program, with an emphasis upon the joy to be found in such work. A basic book for all congregations seeking to follow Jesus' command to let the little children come to Him.

Anita Reith Stohs
Author and Christian Education Consultant

BLUEPRINTS for Children's MINISTRY

CONCORDIA PUBLISHING HOUSE · SAINT LOUIS

Kim E. Bestian

This book is dedicated to Jesus, my Good Shepherd, with whom I am His lamb and ever glad at heart!

Thanksgiving and glory to God for providing me with congregations, parents, children, colleagues, friends, and family to observe, learn from, and work with to make this book possible to be a blessing to others.

Kim E. Bestian

Published by Concordia Publishing House
3558 S. Jefferson Ave., St. Louis, MO 63118–3968
1-800-325-3040 • www.cph.org

Written by Kim E. Bestian

Unless otherwise noted all artwork © iStock / Frank Rampspott

Unless otherwise indicated, Scripture quotations are from the ESV® Bible (The Holy Bible, English Standard Version®), copyright © 2001 by Crossway, a publishing ministry of Good News Publishers. Used by permission. All rights reserved.

Scripture quotations marked NIV are taken from the Holy Bible, New International Version®. NIV®. Copyright © 1973, 1978, 1984 by Biblica, Inc.™ Used by permission of Zondervan. All rights reserved.

Catechism quotations are from *Luther's Small Catechism with Explanation*, copyright © 1986, 1991 Concordia Publishing House. All rights reserved.

Manufactured in the United States of America

Library of Congress Cataloging-in-Publication Data

Names: Bestian, Kim, author.
Title: Blueprints for children's ministry / Kim Bestian.
Description: St. Louis : Concordia Publishing House, 2017.
Identifiers: LCCN 2016051054 | ISBN 9780758657305
Subjects: LCSH: Church work with children.
Classification: LCC BV639.C4 B49 2017 | DDC 259/.22--dc23 LC record available
at https://lccn.loc.gov/2016051054

1 2 3 4 5 6 7 8 9 10   26 25 24 23 22 21 20 19 18 17

CONTENTS

Introduction

Ever since I was a little girl, I have loved the Lord's Church. I remember going to church on Sunday mornings, sitting in the pew, and thinking I was in the King's castle. I felt like a princess wearing my shiny black patent leather shoes. My miniature stuffed gray dog came along with me in my little purse. I would take him out during the sermon to listen to God's Word. When it was time for the offering, my father gave me a dime to put in the plate. First, I put the dime in the palm of my hand and pressed down on it with the thumb from my other hand. As the offering plate passed by, I'd put my gift to Jesus in the plate and then look at my palm where I had pressed the dime down. The imprint of a circle would be left in my hand, and I was reminded that God was always with me.

The Christmas I was four years old will remain a lasting memory. My family and I lived in St. Louis, Missouri, where my father was a teacher in a Lutheran school. For the Christmas Eve service, my Sunday School class had to stand in the front of the church before everyone and sing "As Each Happy Christmas." (I thought we were singing "Azzy Chappy Christmas" and that the song had something to do with chapped lips!) Standing at the end of the line of children by the colorfully lit Christmas tree, I could see the reflection of the tree lights on my shoes. I don't remember singing a word, but I do remember thinking this was the most wonderful thing in the whole world. After the service, we went back to our classrooms to receive a little gift from our teachers. Mine was a small wooden plaque with two lambs painted on it that glowed in the dark. The words said, "The Lord is my Shepherd." Ever since, I have had a fondness for lambs. I still have that plaque to this day, including a large collection of stuffed toy sheep.

Growing up at home, I loved *The Children's Bible* by Anne de Vries, published by Concordia Publishing House. The stories came alive for me. They were impressed upon my heart as my mother read them at bedtime. Homemade felt banners hanging in our dining room marked Church Year celebrations and baptismal birthdays. Family devotions after the dinner meal held inspiring worship and faith-enriching moments. Many of those devotions were from *Little Visits with God* by Allan Hart Jahsmann and Martin P. Simon, also published by Concordia Publishing House. I learned to follow Jesus as our family daily met with God. To help me memorize Bible passages, my father would have me paint with watercolors on large poster paper the meanings of the words and explain them to him. At the time, little did I know how this would affect my life as an adult and enable me to pass these formative treasures on to others.

As a sophomore in high school, I began teaching preschool Sunday School (nursery in those days) at our church in Minnesota. Giving puppet skits for the young ones and sharing the awesome stories of Jesus were dear to my heart. To share what we were learning and doing in Sunday School, I mimeographed letters for the parents. What a joy to sing songs to Jesus with the children and do finger plays to help them remember our Bible verse for the day! I was also active in my church youth group, and the props we fabricated for Vacation Bible School made sweet memories and continued to inspire me as I taught children God's Word.

Soon the time came for college. My desire was to share the light of Jesus with children. I felt drawn to Sunday School, Vacation Bible School, Christmas services, children's choirs, tools that would encourage parents to have family devotions, and so on. That is where my heart's passion was leading me. But in those days, there was no such thing as full-time chil-

dren's ministry, at least in the ways we know it today. I thought about what would be the closest career to doing those things as a church professional and decided to be trained for Lutheran elementary school teaching.

My favorite subject to teach was religion class. I found myself applying Scripture throughout the day with my students. What a joy it was to plan chapel services and prepare the children to sing in church. Those six years of teaching flew! During that time, I married my college sweetheart. He attended seminary and became a pastor. It was wonderful to think about serving the Lord together in His Church.

The first two congregations where God called my husband to shepherd His people did not have a Lutheran school, nor were there any for miles around. But I enjoyed participating in Sunday School, Vacation Bible School, and children's choirs. During that time,

Our life held valleys as well as mountaintops that one finds in church work, but by looking to Christ, trusting in God, and being quick to forgive, I can count it all joy and a great privilege.

our family grew with children of our own. We were blessed with a girl and two boys. The Lord was taking me on new adventures, and I loved every minute of it. Our life held valleys as well as mountaintops that one finds in church work, but by looking to Christ, trusting in God, and being quick to forgive, I can count it all joy and a great privilege.

Our fourth congregation seemed to have a little bit of the personalities of each of our previous three. During our second year there, I was asked to become their first Director of Children's Ministry. For seven years, I loved doing all the things I had felt the Lord preparing and calling me to do in my life. I could hardly wait to get to work each day. My office was my favorite place to pray and create. We had amazing volunteers with awesome gifts that the Lord had given them to use.

It didn't take long until I discovered the need for congregations to have some clarification of what *children's ministry* really means. I discovered that many congregational leaders thought children's ministry consisted only of ordering Sunday School curriculum and supplies, getting volunteers to help, and planning one event after another. They were not clear on what was at the heart of children's ministry, which is much more than finding teachers to teach Sunday School and organizing programs. I began to see that only

when a clear definition of children's ministry emerged would congregations be able to put real value on staffing needs and acknowledge the importance of providing this ministry.

Being involved with other Directors of Children's Ministry in a children's ministry community network and watching other church denominations rapidly lay off these directors, especially because of finances, made it even more evident to me that many churches do not understand the value of a gifted and trained church worker in this area. Because of this, more responsibility is put back on pastors whose time is already stretched thin.

So, the question kept coming to mind, "What is children's ministry?" I had a job description, but it never clearly defined children's ministry. After many experiences, research, and digging deep into Scripture, I found clues that helped me define children's ministry in a way that satisfied my yearning. It is important not only for Directors of Children's Ministry or Children's Ministry Leaders but also for the congregations they serve to understand what children's ministry is and why it is important. Goals can be achieved if the members of a congregation and those who serve the Lord in children's ministry have the same expectations, understanding, and focus.

God provided me various and diverse experienc-

One of my greatest jOYS on earth is to
hear children proclaim, "I can't wait to be there!"

es in my life. He led me down the paths that He chose in order to teach me His ways. He created me and sustained me through many times of testing and trials. He seeded me with the passion of sharing His love with children and with those who minister to them. There have been tears of sorrow and triumphs of success, all of which have formed my character in order to glorify Him. This He does with all those He loves and who follow as His disciples.

REPRODUCIBLE BLUEPRINT

To get started and review blueprints for your own children's ministry, turn to the back of this book for many examples!

God has now allowed me the time to share *Blueprints for Children's Ministry* with you. One of my greatest joys on earth is to hear children proclaim, "I can't wait to be there!" Therein lies the inspiration for defining and creating these Blueprints for Children's Ministry. It is my prayer that this book will give you insight and inspiration for building within His kingdom for those little ones so precious to our dear Savior.

CHAPTER 1

Vision for Children's Ministry Construction

Who are these little people called "children"?
Why build a children's ministry?

As we begin to cast a vision for constructing a children's ministry, we will want to first get to know and understand who children are and why a congregation will want to provide this service. Let's walk through a typical timeline of common occurrences and consider the physical, emotional, and spiritual needs of children as they grow. As we meet these little ones, we will discover the importance of parents and churches partnering together with the Holy Spirit to build a firm foundation for children.

God uses a man and woman together to begin the very start of a new life. Our heavenly Father values this newly created child, endowed with a soul. He or she is lovingly knit together in the secret place inside the mother. The psalmist says it best: "For You formed my inward parts; You knitted me together in my mother's womb. I praise You, for I am fearfully and wonderfully made" (Psalm 139:13–14). In a short amount of time, this baby grows in leaps and bounds. Feeling the little one kick and move is a highlight of great proportion. Anticipation mounts!

Scripture reveals things about our beginnings. Psalm 51:5 states, "Behold, I was brought forth in iniquity, and in sin did my mother conceive me." In Psalm 58:3, we read, "The wicked are estranged from the womb; they go astray from birth, speaking lies." In other words, from the moment of conception, we are in need of our Savior!

Patiently, we wait as the child grows in the womb. God is preparing this little one to enter the world outside of his or her mother. Nine months may seem like a long time for God to work, especially considering He made the whole world in just six days. Perhaps this length of time is not just for the benefit of the baby, but also for the sake of the parents—giving them ample time to get ready. After all, the mother herself requires the necessary time to grow close and connect in love and care with her unseen baby, and the child needs the utmost protection and nourishment from the mother while he or she grows. Even the father requires time to prepare his heart and mind. He needs to get used to the idea of sharing his wife's attention, providing for another mouth to feed, and giving his love to a new little one. In His infinite wisdom, God knows all of this. So, He lovingly provides what is needed. After all, this whole idea was His!

From apples to alcoholic beverages, everything a mother consumes directly affects the development of her unborn baby. God has made it possible for His little child to also experience its mother's emotions. He or she hears talking, noises, laughter, music, and so forth. The little one becomes familiar with the sound of voices in the family and others as it grows inside his or her mother. When our youngest child was just born, he cried so hard. The doctor and nurses could not calm him down. Then, my husband, his daddy, walked over to where he lay, and said his name followed by soothing, fatherly words. Our little one instantly stopped crying. It amazed us all. He recognized his father's voice. He felt safe and secure. Isn't that how we feel when we are sad or sick? We want to cry. We are afraid and unsure. We need the comfort of hearing our heavenly Father's familiar voice. We hear His voice in His Word. This brings us His peace, relief, calmness, and a desire to follow Him. The apostle John reminds us of our Good Shepherd when he writes, "The sheep hear his voice, and he calls his own sheep by name and leads them out. When he has brought out all his own, he goes before them, and the sheep follow him, for they know his voice" (John 10:3–4).

The mysteries of the womb go far beyond what we know. An unborn fetus, regardless of what the world asserts, is a child. Many things influence and affect children from the beginning of their existence. We stand amazed about John the Baptist being filled with the Holy Spirit and leaping for joy in Elizabeth's womb when Jesus' mother, Mary, came to visit. Record of this event is in Luke 1:39–41: "In those days Mary arose and went with haste into the hill country, to a town in Judah, and she entered the house of Zechariah and greeted Elizabeth. And when Elizabeth heard the greeting of Mary, the baby leaped in her womb."

Great rejoicing occurs when a child enters the world. Everyone wants to see and hold the infant—so cute, so soft, so cuddly, so warm and precious. People want to know the child's name and weight and length. I once heard a story about a child looking at a photo album with his mother. The little boy was enthralled at seeing pictures of his first moments after birth. When his mother told him the date he was born, his eyes got so big as he exclaimed, "That's the same day as my birthday!" All the wonderment, discoveries, and connections are amazing to watch as a child explores and learns about the world around him or her.

We find even more joy when the child is "born again" (literally from the Greek, "born from above," John 3:3) and enters the kingdom of God at his or her Baptism. When children are baptized, new life is theirs, and they become our brothers and sisters in Christ— equal in the sight of God. Christian parents and church members follow what it says in Psalm 78:4–7: "We will not hide them from their children, but tell to the coming generation the glorious deeds of the LORD, and His might, and the wonders that He has done. He established a testimony in Jacob and appointed a law in Israel, which He commanded our fathers to teach to their children, that the next generation might know them, the children yet unborn, and arise and tell them to their children, so that they should set their hope in God and not forget the works of God, but keep His commandments." Every child needs to be taught what God has done, what He continues to do today, His great love for them, and what He expects of them. Every child needs a relationship with Jesus. Working through Word and Sacrament, the Holy Spirit creates the gift of faith in hearts. Through His Church, the Holy Spirit continues to strengthen that faith. That is why it is so important for parents and the church to partner together in the life of each child.

God has a great purpose for every child's life—no matter how long or short it may be here on earth. The Lord has specific plans for them all. Through the prophet Jeremiah, God states to His people, "For I know the plans I have for you, declares the LORD, plans for welfare and not for evil, to give you a future and a hope" (Jeremiah 29:11). Children are created to be who God created them to be and not what the world tries to make them.

It has been said that children are like sponges. They soak up lots of information around them. Everything is new to them, inviting, and ready to be "taken in" to their little minds. They are built for learning and doing. Their eyes are wide open for discovery. They not only "soak up" but also mimic everything they hear and see, including the things they hear and see in church. Parents have a necessary role in this development. For example, they can help their children by showing them how to hold a bulletin, how to fold their hands during the Lord's Prayer, and how to give an offering. Children can hum during a hymn even if they can't read the words. Such positive behavior is equally reinforced as the children observe these things in fellow worshipers around them.

Thus, children watch people who are close to them. As already mentioned, this includes people they see at church who interact with them. The relationships children have at church become a prominent part of their family circle. It is a wonderful blessing to witness congregational members come alongside the military mother of four, whose husband is deployed. They start up thoughtful conversations with her, assist her with her children in worship, and even walk out to the church parking lot to help get those little ones buckled up in their car seats. Caring actions like

The **relationships** children have at church become a prominent part of their **family** circle.

© iStock

these communicate silent messages of love not only to the mother but also to her children.

Interaction with others, new discoveries, trust, emotion, motivation, sharing, kindness, and so forth are all things to be considered when dealing with a child. Remember we were once children too. What do you remember about how you felt as a child? What are some things you experienced when you were young that have stuck with you all your life? Who inspired you? Who did you look up to that you wanted to emulate? Whose lap did you want to crawl up into and sit for a while? When did you feel most happy?

Do you remember how you were treated as a child? When you were hurt, were you shown mercy and compassion? (We know that "owies" are a big deal for little ones!) If so, you probably became a compassionate and caring adult. Children will either learn about mercy and compassion, or they will learn not to care for others, depending upon how they were treated. There are many more examples, but the point is the same. How people, especially their parents, respond to children will be how children respond to others. The way life is modeled to a child will be how the child learns to act and respond.

A toddler once dropped a cup on the floor. Her fatigued father kept picking it up and placing it back on her high chair. He became frustrated and sternly said, "Why did you drop that on the floor?" The child's mother intervened and asked the father why he was so upset. He responded, "It's common sense that you don't drop a cup on the floor." This compassionate mother had to remind her irritated husband, "Children at this age do not have common sense yet. I know it is annoying, but she is still learning common sense,

SAFE PLACES

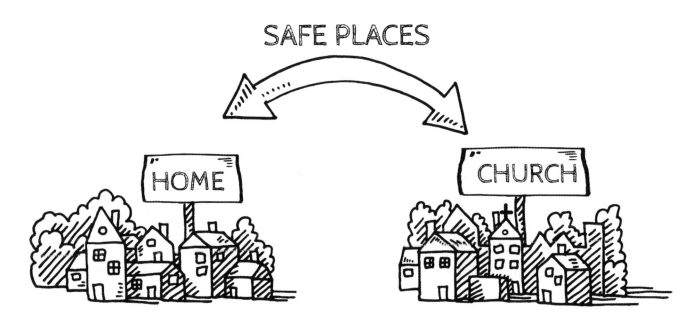

Both a child's home and church home should be
safe places for the child to learn, grow, be loved, and love.

and this is how children learn. She also knows you will keep picking it up for her, so it becomes a game that she is playing with you."

Kids love to run around in the church building. Parents or church members lovingly remind them to walk so they don't fall or knock someone down. These two examples of dropping cups and running in halls may seem like common sense to us, but children need to learn or be reminded of things that are not yet common sense to them. Sometimes they forget and need a gentle reminder too. This is why manners are taught—church manners as well. Children approach new discoveries with experimentation to find out information for future reference and reaction. When interacting with children, just like adults, it is good to be a quick forgiver and to be helpful by speaking kindly, or as Scripture says, "speaking the truth in love" (Ephesians 4:15). Both a child's home and church home should be safe places for the child to learn, grow, be loved, and love.

Repetition is key for children. It enables them to learn and to retain for memory. That's why young children will do things over and over, listen to a song repeatedly, and read the same book time and time again. Children also learn through play. Parents can use these opportunities to teach their children about God's love and His commandments in fun and interactive ways. Through play and repetition, this learning is deeply impressed on them for the rest of their lives. Learning about Jesus through play will help things stick with them. An example would be at Christmas time. Parents might have their child pretend to be Jesus' mommy (Mary) or daddy (Joseph) and rock the baby Jesus (doll). Or they might gather all their child's stuffed animals together and pretend to be Adam, naming all the animals that God made.

This can happen at church as well. If a church provides a two-year-old Sunday School class with parents, trained volunteer teachers can incorporate play into their lessons. It is an added bonus for the child to parallel play and learn about God with other children. They come to recognize that others their age know their best friend, Jesus, too. The parents can also glean ideas of things to do and useful words to speak with their child as they bring them up in the fear and love of God.

Parents are instrumental in helping their child learn to identify and talk about their emotions. This may include the feelings that come with loss. When they comfort their child, it helps the child to better cope with his or her new experience. The child learns that these feelings are normal. Remember that even anger is an acceptable emotion, at times. Scripture simply warns us to not let our anger lead us to sin. Ephesians 4:26–27 says, "Be angry and do not sin; do not let the sun go down on your anger, and give no opportunity to the devil." Loss and anger are only two basic emotions. Many more emotions exist, which provides opportunities for parents to guide their children. Romans 12:15 tells us, "Rejoice with those who rejoice, weep with those who weep." Here we recognize care for others by sharing in their emotions. Even happy emotions are to be shared with each other! What better place to experience and learn about emotions than in the safe environment of the home and the community of saints?

It is important to be tender and understanding as we care for and interact with children. We can easily forget how impressionable they are. Impressions made on a child will leave a deep imprint! Children are down-to-earth and simplistic in their thinking. How children think is different from how adults think. Therefore, we have to rethink the way we talk, teach, and guide them. Introducing a child to a new thought, concept, or Bible lesson could be compared to an adult traveling to a new country with a different language or even visiting another planet without gravity.

Patience is required. Take your time. Thinking from a child's point of view will help you connect with children and enhance their learning. They are simple and humble. They are children, not little adults. They think differently because they have not yet experienced life the way an adult has.

In the Book of Genesis, we read how God tenderly molded Adam from the dust or clay of the ground. Imagine that a child is a lump of clay being molded just like Adam. In fact, Isaiah calls God our potter, acknowledging that we are the clay. Clay gets pinched and pushed and formed in all directions by its potter. All the experiences children have from the very start make up who they will become—just like a lump of clay is formed into a magnificent piece of art. If parents, together with the church, make good impressions on little children, these children will grow up with good experiences and memories of their nurture in the faith. This can strengthen their hearts for God as they will become spiritual leaders in the Church and continue making disciples of all nations. By God's grace, these children will also raise their children to know God and follow Him.

Many parents are exhausted, fearful of being judged, and deep down genuinely concerned if they are doing the right things for their children. They are overwhelmed by their responsibilities of protecting their children and supporting them financially. Add to this the fact that godly parents are the first faith influencers. These responsibilities can easily arouse

Many parents are **exhausted**, **fearful** of being **judged**, and deep down genuinely concerned if they are doing the right things for their children. They are overwhelmed by their responsibilities of protecting their children and supporting them financially.

feelings of anxiety in any parent! The Church is there to support and help them trust in God, to partner with them in teaching God's commands to their children, and to abundantly encourage them. Everyone will then be able to proclaim, "But now, O LORD, You are our Father; we are the clay, and You are our potter; we are all the work of Your hand" (Isaiah 64:8). Blessed are the parents whose congregation partners with them to raise their children in the faith!

As children continue to grow and learn, they may develop a good foundation, but they will still need their godly parents and lots of nurture, guidance, love, and support. Boundaries need to be set from early on, and discipline needs follow-through. Manners, compassion, and generosity are both taught and modeled. Encouragement needs to be mixed with support, understanding, confession, and forgiveness. Through the Holy Spirit, children have the desire to learn about Jesus, obey Him, love others, and express their faith.

Look how Jesus welcomed children in Luke 18:15–17. "Now they were bringing even infants to Him that He might touch them. And when the disciples saw it, they rebuked them. But Jesus called them to Him, saying, 'Let the children come to Me, and do not hinder them, for to such belongs the kingdom of God. Truly, I say to you, whoever does not receive the kingdom of God like a child shall not enter it.'" Again, watch how Jesus rejoices in His Father's will in Luke 10:21: "In that same hour He rejoiced in the Holy Spirit and said, "I thank You, Father, Lord of heaven and earth, that You have hidden these things from the wise and understanding and revealed them to little children; yes, Father, for such was Your gracious will.'" Children are a "big deal" in the sight of God. He wants them to come to Him!

So, why build a children's ministry in your congregation? Children of God are a part of the community of saints. Our heavenly Father values children, so we also should value them. Jesus gave the Great Commission to His Church to make disciples of all nations, which includes children. We are to lovingly obey this command. Children's ministry teaches God's little saints about their heavenly Father and offers opportunities to express and to grow in their faith. Children are people who are at the most impressionable stage of their lives. That is when the Church has the greatest opportunity to influence them spiritually. Let's not take this lightly!

So, why build a children's ministry in your congregation?...

Jesus gave the Great Commission to His Church to make disciples of all nations, which includes children.

Children's ministry helps parents with their responsibility of building lifelong followers of Jesus. The children's ministry program can provide children experiences and situations for learning and faith building that parents appreciate. This gives their children additional opportunities to learn and grow in a faith-focused environment. The congregation supports and reiterates the parents' teaching about God and partners with them as a blessing to families. Christian families are foundational to the Church because families are first to teach of Jesus Christ, our faith's foundation. When the love of Jesus becomes the driving force for parents to raise godly children, the Church is there to partner with them.

The Church also needs children. Children are trusting and unpretentious. When Jesus' disciples asked Him who was the greatest in the kingdom of heaven, Jesus set a little child in their midst. This account is in chapter eighteen of Matthew: "At that time the disciples came to Jesus, saying, 'Who is the greatest in the kingdom of heaven?' And calling to Him a child, He put him in the midst of them and said, 'Truly, I say to you, unless you turn and become like children, you will never enter the kingdom of heaven. Whoever humbles himself like this child is the greatest in the kingdom of heaven. Whoever receives one such child in My name receives Me'" (vv. 1–5). Jesus warns us not to look down upon children. They are precious in His sight! Jesus tells us in Matthew 18:10, "See that you do not despise one of these little ones. For I tell you that in heaven their angels always see the face of My Father who is in heaven." Some translations of this verse actually use the words "do not look down on." Children are one of the greatest examples of faith. The congregation needs them for looking up to as models to be "like," as Jesus acknowledged.

Jesus loves children. I love children. You do, too, or you wouldn't be reading this book. Young ones are like tiny tender plants sprouting upward. They need, and they give.

May God work through you and your congregation to establish, construct, or strengthen your children's ministry!

Children are one of the greatest examples of faith. The congregation needs them for looking up to as models to be "like," as Jesus acknowledged.

The Building Permit and Foundation

CHAPTER 2

What is children's ministry?

How does a church begin building this activity?

When we look outside, we can see that most buildings generally look different. Each one is constructed for a specific need. Stores, restaurants, hospitals, businesses, schools, and so forth are built to house the needs of those they hold. They may look different from the ground up, but they all have similar, if not the same, city-coded rules and regulations for the building of their foundations. Such building codes protect those in the finished building, ensuring safety, endurance, and compliance with the purpose of the building. And let us not forget about the building permit!

Children's ministry is created, or "built," and maintained in very much the same way. There is a basic core beginning, foundation, for each congregation. "But Jesus called them to Him, saying, 'Let the children come to Me, and do not hinder them, for to such belongs the kingdom of God'" (Luke 18:16). The regulations don't come from city hall but from our Lord. "Unless the Lord builds the house, those who build it labor in vain" (Psalm 127:1). And every church already has a permit that we find in Scripture, which we can think of as the "go" part of Matthew 28:19–20. "Go therefore and make disciples of all nations, baptizing them in the name of the Father and of the Son and of the Holy Spirit, teaching them to observe all that I have commanded you. And behold, I am with you always, to the end of the age."

A solid foundation is crucial. Since Jesus is the cornerstone of every church, the rest of the building can be built with confidence. "So then you are no longer strangers and aliens, but you are fellow citizens with the saints and members of the household of God, built on the foundation of the apostles and prophets, Christ Jesus Himself being the cornerstone, in whom the whole structure, being joined together, grows into a holy temple in the Lord. In Him you also are being built together into a dwelling place for God by the Spirit" (Ephesians 2:19–22). Each church must determine its plans of direction for building its ministry through prayer—earnest and continual prayer every day. Don't just think about your building plans in your head. Have actual conversations with God and rely on His Word and

the Holy Spirit for guidance. Here is where a God-directed blueprint is "constructive." Remain grounded in the Bible, turning to Scripture to learn God's will for you and the congregation you serve.

Preparing the Blueprints

Blueprints show you *what*, *where*, *why*, and *how* to build something. They are detailed outlines and plans. Most of us are familiar with blueprints. A blueprint is a photographic print or copy of an architect's drawing with white lines on a blue background. In other words, it is like a map for builders that guides them in the construction of a building.

Blueprints for Children's Ministry are, first and foremost, spiritual in nature. It is God who is the architect. The Holy Spirit leads His people just like the white lines on a blueprint lead the builders. In the Church, white reminds us of purity and holiness. These white lines of direction are then appropriate to think about how the Holy Spirit directs us. The color blue in the Church is used as a reminder of heaven. It is fitting that we think about these Children's Ministry Blueprints as having an earthly purpose for a heavenly goal.

When gathering builders who will help build your church's children's ministry, be sure to define the terms and words that you will be using. Clear definitions make a difference when establishing your ministry. The same focus needs to be understood and agreed upon before any construction work can begin. This will help to maintain harmony and cooperation among the builders. Then watch God do amazing things through His builders!

REPRODUCIBLE BLUEPRINT

To get started and review blueprints for your own children's ministry, turn to the back of this book for many examples!

Before we move on to digging in and preparing the foundation, I'd like to make an important distinction. There are some groups who are leaning toward renaming children's ministry to family ministry. Those two ministries are not the same. *Family* can be a very broad term that when defined includes all ages in the family circle. Teens, grandparents, and others are included in that group. That would pretty much include the whole church because almost everyone in a church is a part of a family. Sometimes, children's ministry and youth ministry will overlap and work together to reach a certain goal. One example would be the family Christmas worship service. When a church offers children's ministry and youth ministry, it is simply dividing Christian education and serving opportunities by age appropriateness. Parents are a part of both those ministries.

Family ministry connects all ages together in Christian education, worship, and service to our Lord. That is the *family* as a whole. Family counseling is just that—counseling! Some churches offer this specialized service as their "family ministry." It exists to help families in their relationships with one another as society uses the term *family*. That would be a ministry *to* families—serving them, not families doing ministry. That is another topic!

In this book, the term "children" will refer to those from birth through sixth grade. However, each congregation will have to determine their own age levels. Seventh and eighth graders are typically considered middle school or junior high school youth. Some churches also include confirmation class as a part of that age group. Sixth graders are often grouped differently based upon the organization of their local school system. Keep in mind that some Sunday School curricula keep fifth and sixth grades together. Congregations that do so come up with unique names for this group—examples include Preteens, TEAM 56, The 56 Club, etc. Other congregations place sixth graders in with the junior youth. Youth in ninth through twelfth grades are generally referred to as the senior high youth group. Again, that is something for each individual church to determine as to what will be best suited for the children and youth of their congregation. Often, congregations determine

© iStock

this by the number of kids in each grade. Sometimes, "critical mass" is important. If there is only one child or very few children in a group, they may benefit by being moved to a class above or below for the sake of friendship among the community of saints.

The "Who" of Children's Ministry

Identifying who the children are in your congregation is essential. It is useful to create a children's ministry directory by listing out those who are of children's ministry age. Knowing who the children are helps in determining what ministries are necessary and for what age groups. Additionally, Sunday School teachers will find this directory useful as their class rosters. They can use it to contact parents and know when to celebrate students' birthdays and baptismal birthdays. Start the directory with newborns and keep the list divided by age or grade levels. To your list add birth dates, baptismal dates, parents' names, addresses, and phone numbers. As you gather this information, also include a question to parents about their privacy preferences. Compile all that information into a booklet form. An easy way to create such a booklet would be to fold 8½ × 11-inch sheets of paper in half for a user-friendly size. For the front cover of the directory, use a logo designed by one of the children in the congregation, or use the year's theme from rally day on the front with its logo, name of church, and the year. Begin the booklet with a brief explanation of children's ministry or a special note from the Director of Children's Ministry. Add short biographies of child ministry volunteers so parents can get to know the ones who are serving their children. Update the directory once or twice a year as needed so as to include children who have been recently born, children who newly joined the church during the past year, or children who advanced to new grades. The term *parents* is an all-inclusive word, because it includes both parents (single or married), stepparents, foster parents, or any other adults who are guardians or caregivers of children.

Hand out a children's ministry directory to each parent whose child is listed in the book. Parents will have a visual reminder then that they are a part of a church family. They will see that their church cares about their family and find it valuable for discovering who else is their child's age. It also serves as a way for parents to know the names of other parents and be able to invite their children to special events such as birthday parties or playtime. Here we see opportunities for fellowship and relationships to form. For the protection of children and their families, do not leave copies out for just anyone to pick up and peruse.

Narrowing the Focus, Defining the Terms

The following are a few terms and their definitions for children's ministry. Once these definitions are clarified and understood, a congregation will be able to work together in unity on the plans to be constructed. God's Word, along with clearly defined terms, will set the foundation. Upon this, a church can build an influential children's ministry!

Definitions

Children's ministry—Children learning about God, following Jesus, and serving Him—children participating actively in the Church's mission and ministry.

Children's ministry program—Planning and setting up opportunities for children first to learn about God and then providing opportunities to serve Him by living out what they have learned; at the same time helping parents build their children to be lifelong disciples of Christ.

Child ministry—A service given by those who serve the Lord by serving children.

Child ministry program—Training, instructing, and equipping people to serve children by teaching, directing, leading, assisting, coordinating, caregiving, and providing any other service needed to serve children so that the children can do ministry.

Having established the definitions, we can now expand on them.

Children's Ministry

Children's ministry is the foundation for youth ministry. If teens have been blessed to grow up in a congregation with a healthy children's ministry, then youth directors or counselors are able to continue to help teens in

their continuing growth of discipleship. They have something to build on! Teens are then introduced to the next step of faith opportunities. This includes intentional witnessing and being able to express the joy of their faith. It also includes an attitude of love, keeping humble and meek in serving. It addresses desired time commitment, discovering spiritual gifts, added responsibilities, and new levels of stewardship and worship.

Christian teenagers will shift from being self-conscious to being confident in Christ. They will move from being self-reliant to trusting in God. Bullying will change to compassion and mercy. Diving deeper into God's Word will strengthen teenagers to follow His commands on moral issues instead of worldly desires and peer pressure. As they grow up in the church, teens can be introduced to how the congregation functions, to the ministry of the church at large, and to their future ministry interests.

Children's ministry involves the young ones becoming disciples. They learn about Jesus, and they follow Him. Learning is their faith nurture, and following is their serving or ministry—putting what they learn into action. Their ministry—their service. All this is cemented together through a relationship with Christ and others. That is the focus. If Christ's disciples, including children, are not given the opportunity to express their faith, even the rocks will cry out (Luke 19:37–40)!

INFANTS AND TODDLERS

A baby needs nourishment from birth. We do not begin feeding our children when they are teens. They need to be fed from day one. Without food, they cannot grow. Children's ministry begins for children *from the time of birth*. Infants are brought to the waters of Holy Baptism, where the

Holy Spirit enters in and begins His divine work. Eternal life begins at Baptism. These little ones are shown God's love and can feel the warmth of it every time they come to church. The babies hear the people pray together and listen to the songs of praise to God. This is children's Christian education at its very beginning.

A Little One's Quiet Room, traditionally referred to as a cry room, is a place for parents to calm a restless baby or change a diaper, or for mothers to nurse. If the quiet room has sound piped in from the sanctuary and some sort of visual to see the congregation, such as a one-way window or a digital screen, worship can continue for the parent and his or her little one. It is a great opportunity for parents to redirect their little toddler to worship and teach about love, reverence, and devotion to God. Consider other ways those so young and dependent can be shown, taught about, and feel God's love in His house. I love the way the New International Version states Psalm 8:2, "Through the praise of children and infants You have established a stronghold."

Infants attending worship is ministry to the church. The parents provide this opportunity. The unspoken messages that children portray are enormous. For example, look how children completely rely on their parents. Like infants, we totally rely on God too. We trust Him for all that He gives us and for all that we need. Infants are both a part of the present and future church. Watch the parents and their influence on their little ones. They set good examples by their attentive worship and prayer.

YOUNG CHILDREN

Parents and parishioners can be positive role models for children. Through observation, the children are learning and laying a solid foundation for a life of worship. Watch closely as young children in church go up with their family for a blessing during Holy Communion. Their eyes are open wide. They witness their fellow older brothers and sisters in Christ  receive Christ's true body and blood. Although they don't fully understand what is happening, they are nonetheless learning that this activity is serious and special. Sometimes we stand when Scripture is read to show honor to God. The children stand too. It is a joy to watch the little ones hold a worship bulletin or hymnal and strive to participate. By their actions, the children are ministering to others. As they attempt to follow, they are setting a wonderful and uplifting example of faith. This is the ministry of little ones!

We need to be gently reminded how important children's ministry is for the church body. Parents are an essential part too. It is easy to forget this. Parents of young children are often overextended and tired, and they may not be able to help teach Sunday School or serve in some other way. One of their most cherished services to the church, however, is bringing their children to God's house. It is great to see members of the congregation reach out to parents and look for ways to help them through words of encouragement, appreciation, and support.

ELEMENTARY CHILDREN

Soon the little ones advance on their spiritual trek from just watching and imitating to cognitively retaining scriptural knowledge. They are now able to start comprehending new concepts. They transition from observation into life application. They begin to intentionally express their faith through their experiences. Just observe their behavior and how they are able to participate in chil-  dren's ministry programs. Children's ministry needs to be held as a top priority in the church. The faith life of a child starts from infancy and sets an enduring foundation. These "seeds" planted in them at a young age will stay with them and have lasting effect on them throughout the rest of their lives. Some habits in life are good and godly. One of those good and godly habits is when parents regularly take their children to worship and Sunday School. Please remember that children cannot drive themselves to church. They are dependent upon their parents to bring them.

If our youth, in their formative years, observe their parents in God's Word, they will be greatly blessed. As they watch their parents in Christian service to others,

These "seeds" planted in them at a young age will stay with them and have lasting effect on them throughout the rest of their lives.

as they continue to be encouraged from Scripture, as they worship with their parents, then they will have been blessed with wonderful role models. They will most likely continue to grow in God's Word and worship. They will want to continue serving the Lord as adults. As Solomon stated so clearly, "Train up a child in the way he should go; even when he is old he will not depart from it" (Proverbs 22:6). Little children—learning God's will and experiencing His love, protection, and guidance—will be filled with joy, contentment, security, and thankfulness. They will want to follow their Savior, Christ Jesus, the rest of their lives.

Children's Ministry Program

A *program* is "a plan of action or agenda." A children's ministry program involves direction and focus. The children's ministry program incorporates three important elements: Christian education, ministry opportunities, and parental relationships. It is necessary to incorporate *play* and *fellowship* inside all three elements of children's ministry. This will enhance the learning process on many levels and ensure relationship building for Christian friendship connections.

CHRISTIAN EDUCATION

The first element is Christian education. Back in chapter one, we acknowledged that what a mother eats and drinks affects her child in the womb. From the moment of birth, the child needs proper nutrition to continue to grow healthy. Faith also needs proper biblical nutrition through Christian education so it, too, can grow. Children are instructed in the Scriptures for the purpose of growing in faith. Instruction includes, but is not limited to, programs such as the Sunday School, Vacation Bible School, Day School, Midweek School, first Communion class, Kids' Night Out—Bible Blast!, and all other Bible classes the church provides for children. This is feeding the lambs! To be a disciple of Jesus means to abide in His teaching, as it says in John 8:31: "So Jesus said to the Jews who had believed Him, "If you abide in My word, you are truly My

disciples." Another translation uses "hold to" in place of "abide." No one, neither children nor adults, can hold to or abide by something that they do not know. That is the reason for Christian education.

Part of Christian education is equipping children to live out their Christian lives. That includes arming them to stand up against persecution—even if they find themselves in a situation that forces them to give up their life for their faith (Matthew 10:22; Ephesians 6:11; Revelation 2:10). How do we do that? We teach the children Bible stories in order to show them heroes of faith and how God works through His people—people who were sinners and in need of His grace; people who struggled and, with God's help, overcame obstacles; people who, by the power of the Spirit, did great things for God and His kingdom.

Bible stories also reveal God as Creator and Sustainer of all things. He is everywhere present with His promises. And He truly keeps His promises and never fails us. He proves that He is faithful to those who follow Him. He instructs us about all of His amazing attributes, such as almighty, unchangeable, eternal, holy, just, loving, faithful, merciful, gracious, benevolent, all-knowing, and so forth.

We teach children that God is the Eternal One, who has our lives planned out for us and that His plans are for our good—to give us "a future and a hope" (Jeremiah 29:11). This gives them knowledge and strength from which to draw in all situations now and in the future. We encourage them to continue growing in the faith by being in God's Word daily. Then, it is the work of the Holy Spirit who will give them the courage to face whatever they must in whatever situation they come up against in their lives.

Thus, learning Bible stories and choosing doctrinally sound curricula are imperative. Teachers need to be properly instructed on how and what to teach in each lesson so that Law and Gospel are presented well. Otherwise, teachers may end up serving their students a deadly dish of moralism. This is all so vital for the spiritual welfare of the young ones and for their faith development. It is a foundational truth on which to build their lives. But! We must first be in God's Word ourselves so that we can know His ways and then impress them truthfully on our children (Deuteronomy 6:4–9).

Scripture reports the story of Mary and Martha in Luke 10:38–42. Mary sat at Jesus' feet—soaking in His every Word. Martha, however, got distracted with the preparation of the meal. Her mind was on everything that had to be done. Martha let fear and worry grip her. She no longer focused on what was really important and even tried to pull her sister away from listening to Jesus. A great Bible passage found in Psalm 46:10 says, "Be still, and know that I am God." We are told to stop what we are doing and trust in God. Listen to Him. We, too, can lose sight of what we really should be doing. We are to be continuously in God's Word. When we are in God's Word, then the Holy Spirit can work in us, filling us with "love, joy, peace, patience, kindness, goodness, faithfulness, gentleness, self-control" (Galatians 5:22–23). When the Holy Spirit grows His fruit in us, we are able to be Jesus' helpers, seeking after things that make an eternal difference. That is being Jesus' disciple. As Jesus' disciples, we shine His light by being who He made us to be! We can desire to provide the best child ministry program for children, but if we focus on the busy nature of the tasks at hand and lose sight of God's Word, we forget that "one thing is necessary" (Luke 10:42).

Sunday School is Christian education in the form of a Bible class geared for children at their levels of learning and concept abilities. This is a fundamental part of children's ministry. Without the feeding of the lambs, there would be no reason to provide the

Teachers need to be properly instructed on how and what to teach in each lesson so that Law and Gospel are presented well.

faith-in-action part. We know that faith without good works and good works without faith are dead. Faith and good works go hand in hand. James 2:14, 17, and 26 read, "What good is it, my brothers, if someone says he has faith but does not have works? Can that faith save him? . . . So also faith by itself, if it does not have works, is dead. . . . For as the body apart from the spirit is dead, so also faith apart from works is dead." When the Bible stories and lessons are taught properly, the Holy Spirit works in the hearts of children so they begin to see and understand the mighty power and love of God. Such Spirit-driven work builds faith, love, trust, and fear in God above all else. The Spirit helps their faith mature so that being helpers for God comes naturally. Faith is the horse and good works is the cart. "We don't put the cart in front of the horse" as one of my college professors often reminded us.

When I taught elementary school, most of the lower grade teachers had one bulletin board dedicated to helpers. This "helping hands" opportunity got the most attention from the children. They could hardly wait to be line leader, bathroom monitor, paper passer, and so on. They longed to be the helper. It was great to be chosen to do something! Children love to help. After learning about the awesomeness of God and His Son, Jesus, children want to share that love with others. It is a real blessing when the church gives children the opportunity to help. Children yearn for this privilege of expressing their faith. When children help others, that is their way of serving or doing ministry. That is their vocation.

Children are taught by us and **learn** about God. The children **become** followers of Jesus by the work of the Holy Spirit. The Holy Spirit is the heart of children's ministry. Then, out of love, the children obey God's Word and **help** others. Therefore we can say that in children's ministry, children **learn, become,** and **help** The **learning** is up to us to share with children. The **becoming** is up to the Holy Spirit. The **helping** is the action of the children that grows out of their learning and becoming. This is the transformation process of a Christian child as they daily develop their discipleship. It's how they **grow** in Christ. Christian children naturally witness their faith and help with the power of the Holy Spirit. The apostle Paul writes in 1 Thessalonians 1:6–7, "And you became imitators of us and of the Lord, for you received the word in much affliction, with the joy of the Holy Spirit, so that you became an example to all the believers in Macedonia and in Achaia."

MINISTRY OPPORTUNITIES

The second important element in the children's ministry program is providing opportunities for children to live out what they have learned on their age-appropriate level. Children listen, learn, and love God and one another. It is their response to God's Word. This response includes living in faith by

- worshiping Him (hear His Word/pray/praise/ give thanks);
- caring for others (share/help/serve);
- sharing their faith (witness); and
- daily living (relationship with God, others).

In other words, children follow Christ and want to be like Him. These things can happen only through the power of the Holy Spirit. Children serve God by loving, caring for, and helping others.

When children build relationships with other children, they are following Jesus in daily living. Sometimes it is hard for children to make friends. They benefit from child ministry volunteers who help them become acquainted and interact with other children. A Sunday School class, for example, made up of a diverse group of children can sometimes have a hard time becoming a cohesive group. A teacher can help

pull them together by finding something they have in common. Even if the only similar thing is that they love Jesus, that can be a powerful uniting factor, which brings them together for friendship, learning, and working together. We do not have to *like* each other, but Jesus does tell us to *love* one another. There is a difference.

Many service opportunities can be offered for children at home and at church with family and friends. These are both protected and safe environments for children. It is best when the parents help and assist their own children with service opportunities in the community or a church family project. As the children become teenagers, church youth groups venture further into this realm of public service projects. Teens are better equipped to face the challenges society brings and to help with greater needs, which exist apart from the church grounds. There are some community and worldwide opportunities appropriate for children, such as mission offerings, food/blanket/toy drives, and the like. Keeping children on the church campus allows for age-appropriate service or "helping" activities without the challenge of field trip permission slips, recruitment of safe drivers with car seats, insurance liability, responsible chaperones, safety concerns regarding strangers, and so on. Children will have plenty of opportunities to experience serving in the world as they grow older. Helping others immediately around them is their first calling when they are very young. Keep service projects age appropriate.

How do children fit into the church's special service events? Church cleanup day? Decorating for Christmas? Vacation Bible School? Congregational Christmas caroling? Preparing for an Easter breakfast? Think of *age-appropriate* things the children can do. For example, children helping the ushers to collect the offering in a worship service may not be age appropriate. But it would be age appropriate for children to help collect the children's offering in Sunday School. Decorating the church Christmas tree could be a great family event. Having the children hang glass ornaments would not be age appropriate for obvious reasons. But having them place felt doves or red ribbons on the tree would be. As children get involved, they will feel a part of their church family, find joy in serving, and establish a solid foundation for years to come. Don't forget: When the children come, the parents come as well! (And vice versa!)

What are other opportunities a church can provide for children to learn and express their faith? What does your church's children's ministry look like? How would you like it to look? Do you even support such a ministry and want it as a part of your church? What are the real needs of the parents in your church to help them disciple their children? What does Jesus say about this? Let's take a moment to review some of God's words in Scripture.

> "When they had finished breakfast, Jesus said to Simon Peter, 'Simon, son of John, do you love Me more than these?' He said to Him, 'Yes, Lord; You know that I love You.' He said to him, 'Feed My lambs.'"
>
> (John 21:15)

This conversation takes place shortly after Peter's denial and the Lord Jesus' resurrection when our Savior met His dejected disciples in Galilee. They had returned there to go fishing. Earlier in His ministry, Jesus said of Peter's confession of faith "on this rock I will build My church" (Matthew 16:18). We recognize that it is God who is the owner of the building. He gives us more than a permit to build. He commands us to build! He also supplies His workers with everything they need. Here, we now see Jesus giving instructions on how to build. He first said to Peter, "Feed My lambs." The church is to provide God's Word as food for growth in faith. Scripture is to be inwardly digested so that it nourishes and produces faith in God's little lambs who are new in the faith.

As **children get involved,** they will feel a part of their church family, **find joy in serving,** and establish a **solid foundation** for years to come.

> "You shall love the LORD your God with all your heart and with all your soul and with all your might. And these words that I command you today shall be on your heart. You shall teach them diligently to your children, and shall talk of them when you sit in your house, and when you walk by the way, and when you lie down, and when you rise. You shall bind them as a sign on your hand, and they shall be as frontlets between your eyes. You shall write them on the doorposts of your house and on your gates."
>
> (Deuteronomy 6:5–9)

Inspired by the Holy Spirit, Moses reminds parents that they are first to wholly love God and then they are responsible for instructing their children in God's ways and about His love. Please notice that it is the parents' responsibility to be in God's Word first. Only then are they able to teach their children about Him.

> "And Jesus came and said to them, 'All authority in heaven and on earth has been given to Me. Go therefore and make disciples of all nations, baptizing them in the name of the Father and of the Son and of the Holy Spirit, teaching them to observe all that I have commanded you. And behold, I am with you always, to the end of the age.'"
>
> (Matthew 28:18-20)

Before Jesus left this soil and ascended to the Father, He instructs His Church to help with this parental responsibility. Please notice carefully to *whom* Jesus is talking in His Great Commission. It is His disciples. They represented the Early Church, the Church of today, and the Church of tomorrow. We are His disciples, too, as we continue to learn from Christ and follow Him. Christ calls us to "make disciples of all nations," which means all people, all ages, and all races. That also includes children. We are to "make disciples" as we go about our daily lives.

Christ's Great Commission applies to both parents and the congregation. It is amazing how God directs both of them to partner together. Parents have the primary responsibility. The church pulls alongside parents to help, equip, support, and encourage them. Being in the process of making young disciples will hold challenges, but God promises to be with us. That is what gives us motivation to keep going. His great love for us gives us the passion to do His work and follow His will. That passion also helps get us through the problems we may face.

Sometimes even children face challenges, such as accepting the differences of others. These differences may include skin color, physical ability, physical appearance, personality traits, and speech impairments. For example, one day in a Sunday School class, many of the children started teasing a fellow student about the thickness of her eyeglasses. It drove her to tears. This presented a teachable moment about kindness and loving others. The teacher was able to share with

We recognize that it is God who is the owner of the building. He gives us more than a permit to build. He commands us to build! He also supplies His workers with everything they need.

the children about being thankful for our eyesight, for doctors, and for glasses to help us see better. Since God has created each one of us and made us unique, adults can help children learn to value one another. This skill will also help children when they are adults in Bible studies, fellowship activities, mission projects, and working side-by-side in the church.

Helping children accept differences is not to be confused with the word *tolerance*. Today, society uses the word *tolerance* to impose the idea that no matter what someone else thinks or believes, everyone should accept them unquestionably without any necessary correction from God's Word. In a postmodern world, this means that anything goes, that there is no right or wrong. However, God calls us not to conform to this world (John 15:8–19; Romans 12:2), but to speak the truth in love (Ephesians 4:15). With the help of the Holy Spirit, parents and the church can show kindness and love while still upholding the truth of God's Word.

PARENTAL RELATIONSHIPS

The third important element in a children's ministry program is maintaining good relationships *with* and *among* parents. Parental relationships are multifaceted. First of all, a healthy and loving relationship must be established between parent and child. Why? Parents, more than any other persons, have the biggest impact on their children. The first responsibility of teaching children about God rests with the parents. Already back in 1525, Martin Luther clearly pointed this out in his Small Catechism. In Section 1 of the Six Chief Parts, Luther writes: "As the head of the family should teach them in a simple way to his household." Parents need to continually be in Scripture themselves so they can impress God's Word on their children. They can introduce Jesus' love to their children already from the time of birth. Parents are to disciple their children and be the primary teachers of faith and Christian role models in their children's lives.

Another aspect of parental relationships is maintaining a supportive connection with the church. The church exists not to teach the children *on behalf of* the parents, but to *reinforce* God's Word, which is to be taught at home. Both the church and the parents are blessed when they work together in this relationship. Children's ministry can provide experiences and help equip parents with resources. This can provide ideas for parents in regard to faith nurture. For example, the church can suggest doing daily family devotions and observing baptismal birthday celebrations. The church can also provide cradle roll flyers that contain stages of development, parenting classes, church newsletter articles on Christian family life, special parent night "family focus" groups with a guest speaker and where family interactive Bible ideas are shared, and so on. Encouraging Christian parents and connecting them with other church moms and dads is a great bonus. They can share common issues and related experiences with one another. They can establish long-lasting friendships. All of this further strengthens the community of saints.

Supporting the parents with information on children's spiritual development, encouraging them to talk to their children often about God, and showing them ways to teach their children on how God demonstrates His love to us is a great gift a church can give its young families. This is building up the family of God.

One of the greatest church-parent challenges is getting families to attend Bible studies and worship with the community of saints *every* Sunday. When the church forms a close bond with parents, then parents will develop a listening ear and a teachable spirit. They will come to recognize that worship is for God and their family. Going to church is not like going to a country club. It is so much more than a mere community group. One of the main reasons the early Christians chose Sunday as the day of worship was in honor of Christ's resurrection. Every Sunday then is meant to be a little Easter celebration. The Holy Spirit convicts parents that the Body of Christ is edified when the members are all together in Bible study, fellowship, and worship of our risen Lord. The presence of parents and their children is needed within the church. It is not only a blessing to the other children, but a blessing to their teachers as well! As children get older and become more involved with sports, faithful Christian parents should hold the conviction that worship and Bible study have priority over a Sunday morning soccer game or practice. They must safeguard Sunday mornings for the sake of their families. Parents may need to talk to their children's coach to explain that family worship is nonnegotiable. Pray for our churches to partner with parents in this way. Pray for parents in our churches to be strong and courageous in the Lord—to hold God's Word sacred and gladly hear it and learn it.

Churches can also offer a Sunday School class for two-year-olds together with their parents. This sends the message to children that God's Word is important even to their mom and dad. It also says, "Dad and Mom love Jesus! They want to come with me to Sunday School so we can pray, sing, and learn about Him." When parents attend Bible class on a Sunday morning while their children are in Sunday School, their children begin to realize that studying God's Word is important for people of all ages. Even as an adult, they will need to continue learning about God. Here again, we see the silent messages that children receive and take to heart by observing their parents.

STEPS IN BUILDING A CHILDREN'S MINISTRY PROGRAM

When constructing a house, first the plumbing is set. The water lines are put in, and then footings have to be dug. Finally, the concrete is poured as the foundation. It is fun to compare the water lines that run to and from a building to our Christian lives. Our foundation begins at Baptism (water lines), which gives new life. Then our sins are taken away, washed from the house. That is the foundation of our Christian life!

After the foundation, the house needs to be framed. When the framing is complete, a contractor installs roof decking, electrical wiring, alarm systems, insulation, roofing, windows, and then all the finishing touches. You can't paint the walls until the drywall has been installed. There is an order to things for particular reasons. There are many details and steps to take. Building supplies have to be ordered. Codes need to be followed. Inspections have to be approved before the next part of the building can be assembled.

Like the world of construction, there are also important steps that need to take place when building a children's ministry. As it was stated earlier, there is an order to things for particular reasons. Each step builds on the previous step.

STEP 1: Pray for the Holy Spirit's guidance; stay rooted in the Word.

STEP 2: Define and communicate key words in children's ministry.

STEP 3: Recognize the three important elements in a children's ministry program. (See p. 20.)

STEP 4: Understand the value of children's ministry.

STEP 5: Agree to provide and support children's ministry.

STEP 6: Set the goal, purpose, objective, mission, and vision for children's ministry.

STEP 7: Determine budget and facility availability.

STEP 8: Establish a Director of Children's Ministry (DCM) or Children's Ministry Leader (CML).

STEP 9: Identify the children in the congregation.

STEP 10: Create blueprints for your children's ministry, including ministry (job) descriptions.

STEP 11: Recruit, prepare, and engage volunteers in child ministry by teaching, training, inspiring, encouraging, and sending.

STEP 12: Give thanks to God and continue to develop the children's ministry.

Once again, please note the order. Step 9 intentionally belongs where it is. The number of children in your congregation should not be the primary reason or determining factor for beginning a children's ministry. No matter how *many* or how *few* children are in your congregation, all children are valued. Once the children are identified, however, specific age-related activities, opportunities, programs, and events are more easily initiated.

Child Ministry

Child ministry is volunteers serving children. Child ministry volunteers look out for the needs of the children entrusted to them. They serve the Lord by serving the children. They provide care and religious instruction for God's little saints. They teach them about God's love and forgiveness. They also assist children in ways that help them to express their faith and serve others. Publishing houses and authors who provide religious resources and curricula are also a part of child ministry. Because of their important role, it is essential that child ministry volunteers first be in God's Word themselves. Being in God's Word is a *daily* event. For any Christian, but especially the child ministry worker, this includes devotions, personal and corporate Bible study, and weekly worship.

A child ministry worker is typically a volunteer (Sunday School teacher) or paid church worker (nursery attendant) *directly* involved with children for the purpose of nurturing the faith of children. It is advised that those who work directly with children have background checks. A person who signs up to open and lock up the building for a children's ministry event, those who take care of registration, people who set up and take down tables and chairs, and individuals who clean up after a program are volunteers who are considered *indirect* child ministry volunteers. What they do still helps to serve children, but they don't necessarily need background checks because they do not work directly with them. The child-care attendant, nursery worker, or babysitter is considered a child ministry worker because that person uses their Christian kindness and shares Jesus' love as they talk with and care for the children. That is why, when seeking a child-care attendant, it is highly advisable that a mature Christian be hired.

Children learn best from teachers whom they admire and who show an interest in them. Child ministry volunteers who develop close relationships with children will be able to have a bigger impact on them. Children are better prepared and ready to listen and learn from someone they know and trust.

Directors and leaders can assist those who do child ministry with ideas about forming relationships with children. Use your children's ministry directory as a starting point. Be sure the child ministry volunteers know the parent's names and the number of siblings

Children learn best from teachers whom they admire and who show an interest in them.

in the family. Remind the teachers to call each child by name and make sure the children know the names of those teaching them. Provide child ministry volunteers with simple questions, which they can use to engage their students and start forming relationships. Here are a few conversation-starter ideas: "What is your favorite color (fruit, animal)? Do you have any pets at home? If so, what are their names? Did anything surprise you this week? Did you meet any new friends? If you were given five bicycles, what would you do with them all? Have you ever gone to a baseball game? Tell me about a time when you were really, really happy/sad." Such questions indicate interest in a child and can present a "teachable moment." A teachable moment is when something is talked about or something unplanned happens that provides the opportunity for a life lesson to be taught.

Child ministry volunteers are blessed when they spend time both listening to and conversing with children. If other children are close by, they, too, can be drawn into the conversation. Be sure to encourage the child ministry volunteers to share about themselves with the youngsters. Building a relationship goes both ways. Children are generally interested in knowing more about their leader, as well as other children. This shared relationship building brings a group close together and sensitizes care for one another. When child ministry volunteers establish good relationships with the children, this will help develop each child's relationship with Jesus and others.

When child ministry volunteers take the time to

make personal home visits, this will make a positive connection with the child and his or her family. Home is the child's safety base. During such visits, parents also are given an opportunity to learn more about their child's teacher, and vice versa. Child ministry volunteers can learn a lot about a family while being in the home environment. It better equips them in understanding the child. When someone enters another's world and shows interest in that person's life, relationships grow deeper.

Can a church provide child ministry with no children's ministry program? The answer is an undeniable yes. Most churches provide a Sunday School for children. Each Sunday, the congregation feeds God's Word to their little ones by teaching them Bible stories and lessons. The church recruits child ministry volunteers to teach the lessons. However, as mentioned earlier, providing Christian education is only one part of the children's ministry program. In order to have a complete children's ministry program, a church would have to provide opportunities for the children to serve and witness their faith—based upon what they have learned. Children's ministry is the action of the children. Notice the apostrophe in the words "children's ministry." It is *their* ministry. It is what they *do*. When churches provide Christian education, the Holy Spirit does His work of changing hearts and moving the children to serve the Lord. A desire develops within them to express their faith. The Holy Spirit is the One who works faith through the hearing of God's Word, which then produces service, or good works. Both child ministry and children's ministry are tied together through the work of the Holy Spirit. The ministry of the Church belongs to Christ, whose Spirit works through His people—children too!—to serve one another.

Whether the church provides opportunities of service for the children or not, the world itself provides many service opportunities. The question is this: Does the church give its children the opportunity to serve? Some churches, spoken or unspoken, ignore their children. Some may see them as simply a necessary nuisance. They do not understand that ministry is something that God calls all of His people to do—including children.

While children's ministry can happen without a children's ministry program, congregations can and should offer a complete children's ministry program package for their children. It will mostly look different for each congregation, and God will use your church to nurture the children He has placed there. After all, we feed our children good food so they can grow and live. When they exercise through play, their body is using the consumed food for physical action. The result is happy, healthy, growing children. When we feed children God's Word and then provide opportunities for the children to exercise their faith through ministry, the result is happy, spiritually healthy, and growing children—full of God's grace and joy!

Child Ministry Program

The child ministry program is a plan that consists of working with your volunteers by equipping them to serve the children. They are like construction workers who use various tools—hammer, saw, measuring tape, and so on. They will benefit from good quality training, guidance, encouragement, and blueprints. We will discuss more of this in the next chapter.

Just a word of caution: Building can be a slow process. One nail at a time! Like that old saying goes, "The mills of the Lord grind exceedingly slow, but grind exceedingly fine." Going fast is not the goal. Building well and for good reason is the aim. Do you remember what happened to the wise man who built his house on a rock (Matthew 7:24–25)? His house stood strong! The key is to build if the need is there, and to be wise about building.

The Builders

Who is going to build?
Where and how should they build?

© iStock / Askold Ramonov

CHAPTER 3

Your TEAM of builders, or child ministry volunteers, will be better able to build a ministry if they all follow the same blueprints. Blueprints are made up of goals, purposes, objectives, activities, and reflections. They show *what*, *why*, *how*, *where*, and *when* to build. As the builders focus on the same goal and for the same reasons, there should be harmony within the team. Everyone should be going in the same direction.

TEAM

Here is a common acronym you have probably seen somewhere before:

Together Everyone Achieves More

There are many TEAMs in which the Director of Children's Ministry has an active and important role. One team is made up of the pastor, the elders, and the Director of Children's Ministry (DCM). As far as children's ministry is concerned, this team cares about the welfare of the DCM, supports and encourages him or her, and reflects on how the children's ministry is developing. They deal with any concerns, needs, and blessings of the ministry in relationship to doctrine and the people involved. Another team is the Board of Children's Ministry. This group makes sure that children's ministry is implemented and well maintained in the congregation. They gather to communicate and reflect on current children's ministry opportunities and new ideas. They work alongside the DCM for vision and planning, and they help obtain volunteer and paid child ministry workers. This TEAM also promotes activities in the children's ministry program.

Whenever there is some type of activity involving volunteer or paid child ministry workers, such a group becomes a team. For example, the Sunday School teachers make up a team. The Vacation Bible School volunteers make up another team—and so forth. A church volunteer team or child ministry team works jointly as the Body of Christ (1 Corinthians 12:12–31) in service for a central purpose.

VOLUNTEERS

Here is a new acronym that I have created to help define the meaning of volunteer:
Very **O**bedient **L**eaders **U**nder **N**oble **T**asks **E**arnestly **E**xperiencing **R**eal **S**ervanthood!

The last section of this book contains sample job descriptions or ministry descriptions for those who do child ministry in the church. Ministry descriptions are used for those in volunteer positions. Job descriptions are typically used for paid or hired positions. But keep in mind that these hired "job" positions are ministry too. Job and ministry descriptions are important so that workers know the expectations of their roles. This eases the anxiety for those contemplating and accepting the task. It also eases frustration, which is caused from not knowing the expectations and what is to be accomplished. Volunteers can see at a glance if they have the gift to achieve what they are being asked to do.

How wonderful that God has blessed His Church with servants who have dedicated hearts and a desire to make disciples by using the gifts He has supplied them. It is brilliant how God decided to give different gifts and talents to various people so that they will have to rely on one another in the Body of Christ. By working together, strong relationships are formed. We all work collectively for the one purpose of making disciples of Jesus Christ.

So, what do you need to look for in a child ministry volunteer? Here are some important traits: A member of the congregation who

- is faithful in Bible study, worship, and prayer.
- loves children and has a passion for their faith development.
- is responsible and trustworthy.
- has a teachable spirit.
- communicates well with children and adults.
- is willing to be a team player.
- is not a recent convert.

In 1 Timothy 3:6, the apostle Paul advises Timothy regarding an overseer in the church. He writes, "He must not be a recent convert, or he may become puffed up with conceit and fall into the condemnation of the devil." Based on Paul's advice, volunteers responsible for instructing children should not be new to the faith or your church's denomination. They need time to grow deeper in the faith and to become more familiar with the church's doctrine. New converts to the faith can be overly excited and have unrealistic expectations. They can be easily offended and influenced by pride. They have a higher chance of leaving the church if something unfortunate (e.g., a tragedy or serious conflict) happens. This could even affect their eternal salvation. Satan loves to visit God's church and disrupt things. (It is important for volunteers to become familiar with the reconciliation process found in Matthew 18:15–35.) For that reason, be cautious before recruiting new Christians to serve as leaders in child ministry.

Think carefully about your purpose when asking certain people to volunteer. Are you asking the same people over and over again? Is it possible for you to ask other people whose potential and service have not yet been utilized? Are you asking too much of your pastor? What are some good reasons for asking the person you are requesting to assist? Look for a volunteer who has interests, talents, and maturity. Examine your motives. Be sure to have good reasons for asking the volunteers you seek.

Putting an article in the church newsletter or an announcement in the worship bulletin asking for Sunday School teachers, for example, can appear cold, uncaring, and desperate. Other problems can arise from this as well. Not everyone has the gift of teaching even if they think they do. There are also those who may have the gift but do not think they are needed.

When searching for teachers, first pray, pray, and then pray some more. Let God lead the way. After all, it is His Church. In your prayers, thank God for providing the necessary servants and gifts to His Church. As the apostle Paul reminds us, "And my God will supply every need of yours according to His riches in glory in Christ Jesus" (Philippians 4:19). And don't forget about Christ's undershepherd of your congregation. It is good to consult your pastor as to who he feels would best fit the needs of your ministry. He knows God's flock and helps lead His sheep. Continue to pray with your Board of Children's Ministry.

A beautiful prayer example for this particular situation is found in Acts 1:24, where Jesus' disciples are needing to find someone to fill Judas's place after Jesus had ascended into heaven: "And they prayed and said, 'You, Lord, who know the hearts of all, show which one of these two You have chosen.'" God knows what is in everyone's heart. We trustingly ask that He would lead us, in His way and in His time, to the person or persons needed. For it is He who chooses us and sets before us good works in advance for us to do.

When approaching people to volunteer, tell each person how wonderful it would be to have him or her on the team. Share the gifts you think he or she has to be a part of the ministry. Communicate the benefits and the excitement of working together in this way. Stay positive. Share with them the gifts you think they have to be a part of the ministry. Let them know what a blessing he or she will be to others. Give a copy of the ministry description. Encourage the person to read through it and pray about involvement. Get back with him or her in a timely manner regarding the decision. No matter what the answer may be, thank him or her for considering. If he or she accepts the position, offer guidance, assistance, and support. Stay by their side. If he or she declines the position, continue to give support and thank them for their consideration.

Volunteers can use a teacher's guide for Sunday School or Vacation Bible School like a builder can use a hammer or a saw. However, they will still need directions and instructions on how to use the materials. Some people require more guidance than others. God calls all kinds of people to do His work, and patience goes a long way in training.

It is good to consult your pastor as to whom he feels would best fit the needs of your ministry. He knows God's flock and helps lead His sheep.

© iStock / Askold Ramonov

It is helpful to have volunteers or child ministry volunteers sign a special agreement form promising to follow sound doctrine to the best of their ability. Titus 2:1 says, "But as for you, teach what accords with sound doctrine." After all, God takes the instruction of His precious little ones very seriously. The Lord Jesus states, "Whoever receives one such child in My name receives Me, but whoever causes one of these little ones who believe in Me to sin, it would be better for him to have a great millstone fastened around his neck and to be drowned in the depth of the sea" (Matthew 18:5–6). A little further on in verse 10, we read, "See that you do not despise one of these little ones. For I tell you that in heaven their angels always see the face of My Father who is in heaven." God deeply loves His children. Remember—with responsibility comes accountability!

Child ministry volunteers are responsible for teaching the doctrine of their church denomination. Be sure your volunteers know where the church stands on theological issues as well as moral issues. Those involved as leaders in child ministry are expected to abide by the theology of the church. Most churches have policies that require that volunteers in a teaching capacity be members of the congregation.

The youth of the church can be valuable assets to the congregation and to child ministry. Some congregations invite teens to help with events that are typically centered on children. Many serve as helpers for programs such as Vacation Bible School. However, even though many teenagers babysit, never assume they know how to properly care for children. It is important to instruct this group of youth on their responsibilities. Some teenagers are more mature than others, so know your volunteers well. Unknowingly, some may send improper silent messages—by the way they act, by the words they use, by the way they

BOUNDARIES

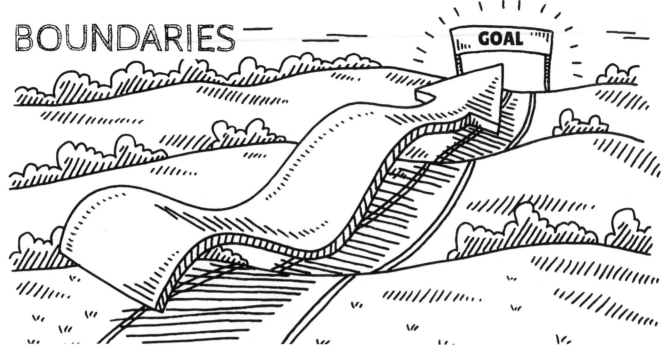

To establish a **strong ministry**, boundaries need to be set in place and be **understood** by everyone involved.

dress—to the young ones. (Even adult volunteers can easily fall into this trap.) Determine which teens are capable of being responsible with children. Be sure to thank them for serving with joy, and let them know that they are greatly appreciated.

Some builders are natural helpers. God has woven it into their DNA. Tell them what to do, and they do it. On the other hand, there are builders who are natural leaders. They were born to be out there in front showing the way. Both types of people, followers and leaders, are needed for the building process. They work well together. However, there can also be challenges. Natural-born helpers can find it difficult and uncomfortable to direct something. And natural-born leaders can become frustrated when they have to follow. It is helpful to observe and take note of who has the gift to follow and who has the gift to lead. Interestingly, if no leader is appointed in a group one will suddenly appear. Just watch!

Boundaries

After a building's foundation has been laid, framework is then added. Framework gives the builders the necessary boundaries on which to build. Boundaries are vital to maintaining the proper size and proportion of the building. The last thing any builder desires is a crooked building. The same idea holds true for your Children's Ministry Blueprints. To establish a strong ministry, boundaries need to be set in place and be understood by everyone involved. If there is a lack of direction, people end up doing what they think is right instead of staying focused on the goal and the partnership of the TEAM. Conflict usually results when competing opinions collide.

For example, a Sunday School teacher doesn't feel comfortable teaching the Bible story for that day, so she decides to do something else. Did she check with the Sunday School Head Coordinator first? Or was this a unilateral decision? This is one reason it is important to hold regular Sunday School meetings. Boundaries need to be established and questions answered. Communication and common sense are useful in preserving boundaries.

Let me share another example. Feelings can be hurt if one child ministry worker interferes with another's task because he or she feels the task is not being properly done. That is not a good approach if there is a concern. Instead, the concerned child ministry volunteer can come alongside the fellow volunteer and ask if he or she would like some help. Again, this is where volunteer training comes in. Training sessions can address these types of issues ahead of time. Job descriptions and ministry descriptions help to define one another's boundaries. Keep the ministry descriptions as clear and simple as possible. If thorny issues arise, be sure to consult with your pastor for wisdom and biblical guidance.

If a classroom is shared with a preschool or elementary school, be sure your volunteers know the boundaries in that room. Respect for equipment is a Christlike attitude valued by others who use the room at other times. Have the child ministry volunteer build an "us" space in a classroom. Prepare a large cardboard trifold with the year's theme listed on the top. Include photos of the students, their names, birthday and baptismal birthday dates, and a photo of the child ministry volunteer and his or her picture. This might also be a great place to include an attendance chart.

If possible, have a special designated place outside the classroom for keeping children's ministry supplies, such as Bibles and crayons, for events or programs. Child ministry volunteers can pick up their supplies before going to the room they will be using. Have a cart with rollers available, which another volunteer can take down the hallway to deliver and pick up supplies. This would be a great job for someone who doesn't have the gift of teaching but would like to help in some way. They could be new to the church and need time to adjust to the program. Even this position would benefit from having a written ministry description.

People like to be creative. Without boundaries, however, creativity may lead some to unintentionally do something that causes offense. People who "take the law into their own hands" can wind up creating an inadvertent mess. They may have good intentions and may even think that they are being helpful. But in reality, they end up creating a dilemma. It could even snowball into a crisis within the church. Explain to volunteers that they should always seek approval or permission before going ahead with a new plan. They will save themselves (and others!) countless headaches and heartaches if they ask first.

Distractions

If a builder becomes distracted during his work, for one reason or another, he may forget to do something crucial, such as nailing down and sealing roof vents. When the rains pour down, the rafters and the insulation under the roof become severely damaged, if not ruined. What a mess this creates for the homeowner. A great deal of repair work is then required. If a builder gets distracted and doesn't properly plan ahead, he will also fail to order ample building supplies. This causes a stressful delay in the home's deadline.

Similar things can happen in child ministry. At times, distractions happen and volunteers start to add to or take away from the overall goal and purpose of the ministry plan. When distractions occur, people lose sight of the intended focus and aim. Sometimes they forget *what* they are doing or *why* they are doing it. They end up doing additional work with no intended purpose. Plan ahead, be prepared, and keep sight of the blueprints!

Distractions come in all shapes and sizes. And Satan applauds when God's people become sidetracked. People may become overextended and overwhelmed. They may fail to delegate when assistance is needed. They may feel that they can do a far better job than anyone else, or it is just easier to do it themselves. As a result, burnout and depression become a reality. This not only harms the worker, but it damages the ministry itself. These and other distractions can hurt those who serve in child ministry, which then hurts the ministry itself.

REPRODUCIBLE BLUEPRINT

To get started and review blueprints for your own children's ministry, turn to the back of this book for many examples!

Blueprints are absolutely indispensable for the progression of the building. They give direction. Child ministry volunteers must focus on the goals, purpose, and objectives of the building, in other words, the child ministry. Blueprints need to be read and reviewed often. If not, your focus will become easily blurred. Memory does not always serve truth. You will have an effective building if the blueprints are followed consistently. When people have direction and know they are valued for their service, they will feel confident and have joy in what they have accomplished.

Determining and Following the Head Foreman

Who will be the administrator or Director of Children's Ministry in your church? Will that person have professional qualifications, gifts, and abilities? Will they be responsible for keeping the ministry in accord with your church's theological stance and mission? Who will train those who do child ministry? How can you prepare for safety and conflict?

Those who do child ministry are blessed in their work if the church provides a strong support system to assist and enable them to carry out their tasks. They will need to be equipped with skills in the teaching and application of Scripture, discipline and reconciliation, and child development and concept levels.

REPRODUCIBLE BLUEPRINT

Turn to the back of the book to see the blueprint for Director of Children's Ministry.

A Director of Children's Ministry is called to oversee the faith nurturing of children in the church. They can create opportunities for children to put their faith into action. Directors help foster and establish relationships not only with children, but also among parents, staff, and volunteers. The Director of Children's Ministry is there to help guard against false doctrine. He or she further equips child ministry volunteers in the understanding and distinction of Law and Gospel. He or she helps child ministry volunteers to avoid the common teaching of moralism. The Director of Children's Ministry is accountable to the pastor of the congregation, who holds the ultimate responsibility for sound doctrine.

Hundreds of resources are available today for churches to use. Not everything these materials endorse or teach is biblically based. Many volunteers, depending on their scriptural knowledge, may have difficulty discerning any differences from their own denomination's confession. A professionally trained church worker can be a great asset to your church. This person should have skills and discernment in this area. That is also why it is important for the director to work closely with the pastor of the congregation. Even though a director has some training, the pastor still has more training and experience in this area. Therefore his advice and counsel should be sought when dealing with uncertain issues of doctrine.

If the Director of Children's Ministry is teacher-trained

© iStock

for a Christian school, the director will have experience in choosing curricula and will be knowledgeable in the concept-levels and age-appropriateness of children. Child development and levels of spiritual concepts also play into this. Directors with teacher training can guide child ministry volunteers when it comes to understanding (not diagnosing) learning challenges in children, such as ADHD, auditory processing disorder, dyslexia, autism, Asperger's syndrome, and so forth. Child ministry volunteers who are well informed about learning styles in the areas of kinetic, visual, and audio will be better equipped to teach Bible lessons to children who learn differently. Emotional sensitivity and age-appropriate abilities can play a big role in the classroom when enrichment activities are used to make a Bible point stick. There are also physical considerations to keep in mind. Do any of the children suffer from diabetes, allergies, asthma, sight or hearing impairment, or obesity? Are there any emotional issues involved? Child ministry meetings become critical for equipping volunteer teachers for service. These meetings can help child ministry volunteers know where to begin in seeking further help with specific topics. Additional information about children with special needs can be found on the Internet. However, be discerning with the information you find. When these developmental and learning issues are encountered, a Director of Children's Ministry will prove to be a great blessing.

Pastors are called by their congregations to shepherd all of God's people, and children are obviously a part of that group. Because of a pastor's countless responsibilities and time constraints, however, a Director of Children's Ministry is another equipped staff member who is able to help deal with the numerous details of children's ministry. They help take some of the responsibilities off the pastor's plate. What a great relief and blessing Directors of Children's Ministry are to pastors and congregations! Christian colleges and universities who help train such church workers and prepare them for ministry are great assets to the Church at large.

But perhaps your congregation does not have the funds to support another church worker such as a Director of Children's Ministry. A volunteer can be chosen to lead the children's ministry and have a title such as Children's Ministry Leader. This person would work closely with the pastor to make sure that the blueprints are administered. Many resources are available to assist Children's Ministry Leaders to grow in their skills. Regular meetings with the pastor are very beneficial. As long as there are blueprints to be followed, their guidelines will allow for continuous building in God's kingdom here on earth.

A child's first personal encounter with the pastor is probably at his or her Baptism. If the child was baptized as an infant, they won't remember the pastor. As the child grows, perhaps the only contact with the pastor is hearing his voice in worship and shaking his hand or giving a high five as they exit at the end of worship. How wonderful for a young child to hear the voice of his or her pastor during a church service. That is why a children's sermon or children's message during worship can be so valuable.

Having an opportunity to learn from the pastor is like a "seed" being planted in the ground of a child's heart. Coming forward to sit with the pastor and interact with him during a children's message can be a positive experience and an important part in relationship building. As they become teens and adults, children will continue to grow on that foundational relationship, which began when they were very young. It will stay with them the rest of their lives. Those "seeds" planted in children are very deep and leave lifelong impressions.

Leading in Love

Through God's guidance, the church provides leaders and sets them in place. These leaders **T**each, **I**nspire, **E**ncourage, and **S**end child ministry volunteers who have a passion for God's little lambs. This **TIES** acronym helps pastors, Directors of Children's Ministry, and Children's Ministry Leaders to remember their primary responsibilities and to prepare workers in children's ministry. This special **TIES** plan is derived from Hosea 11:4, "I led them with cords of kindness, with the bands of love." Other translations use the words, "human kindness, with **ties** of love."

Teach   **Knowledge and skill**
         To deliver information needed for a particular area of learning

Inspire   **Divine influence**
         To cast vision, excite, entice, and motivate into wanting to join in and participate

Encourage   **Reassure and promote**
         To coach and create a sense of approval, confidence, and continuance as support

Send   **Permit and dismiss**
         To enable to go and do all that has been acquired

Because of His great love, God leads us with kindness, satisfies our human needs, and sets an example for us to lead others. Through Christian faith, we share and demonstrate kindness to others and wrap it all up with ties of love, which bind it all together.

Kindness or TIES of love include compassion, consideration, generosity, gentleness, helpfulness, sympathy, thoughtfulness, understanding, and most of all, mercy. Mercy is kindness to someone who doesn't deserve it. Here are some examples of how to incorporate TIES of love in your children's ministry program. The ideas are endless!

- Clear and helpful information at meetings
- Newsletter articles or personal notes that acknowledge and give thanks to those people who are serving
- Personal encounters that show care and interest
- Sympathetic or celebrative moments on the phone
- Snacks at training sessions.

- Kind words and encouragement even if someone is late
- An understanding heart to those who couldn't make a meeting
- Displaying equanimity when there is a frustration or disagreement
- A small gift to a tired soul or even a not-so-tired soul
- Patience and a listening ear
- Plenty of supplies and ideas
- Checks to see that children's books in the library are updated, fresh, and applicable
- Help in preparations
- A praise pat on the back
- Flexibility while collectively creating, planning, and working toward a goal
- Lots of smiles
- Providing Blueprints for Children's Ministry

Above all, lead with love—the way God leads His people with the sort of kindness that we as humans need. "The LORD is my shepherd; I shall not want" (Psalm 23:1). Our Good Shepherd knows our human needs. "But grow in the grace and knowledge of our Lord and Savior Jesus Christ. To Him be the glory both now and to the day of eternity. Amen" (2 Peter 3:18). Therefore, trusting in our Good Shepherd, we grow to give our wanting to His will, so that our leading others will reflect Jesus' love and bring glory to God. Shepherds show love to the sheep by caring for them so that they will want to follow the shepherd. How does that translate for leaders as they encourage people to follow their lead? We go back to the growing in grace and knowledge of Jesus in order for patience and trustworthiness to be valuable attributes found in the leader.

God *leads* us; He does not *manage* us. When a person hears the word *manage*, they tend to think of domination or dictatorship. Management is a force. Managers, in this context, follow rules no matter what.

It is law. They feel safe and comfortable following the strictest of rules. They make and push others to follow their dictates.

Leadership means to guide. It is going first and preparing the way. It is being an example, showing direction, and having a positive influence. Leadership is love. We would much rather have someone lead us than manage us. We submit to God's leadership willingly because it is Jesus who lives in us since our Baptism. We want to follow Him. Management gives no choice. If God managed us, He would force us to follow Him. He does not do that. We want to follow Him because of His great love for us. Jesus calls us sheep. In the animal world, cattle are driven, but sheep cannot be driven. They are "programmed" to follow. Think of ways to connect with people so that they will want to follow.

Many members within our congregations work in the business world. They have learned to manage people. Sometimes, all they know is management. After all, they manage people all day long. Then they volunteer for a church ministry or are elected to serve as chairpersons of church boards. What a challenge it is for managers to learn to become leaders! Often, it is difficult for them to transition from managing to leading in the church. Some may even think that pastors and professional church workers are not good leaders because they do not manage other people. There is a time and place for management and a time and place for leadership. Blessed is the children's ministry where there is loving leadership and not management! Blessed are the child ministry volunteers who humbly submit and follow their God-given leaders!

Psalm 23:2 reminds us, "He leads me beside still waters." Sheep will not drink from rushing water. The water needs to be still for sheep to safely drink. God knows what we humanly need and what is best for us. He does not force us to go to the still waters. Instead, He guides and provides. Such love He has for us! He teaches, inspires, encourages, and sends us, His sheep. We, too, are to follow His example with love.

Sometimes, there will be appointed directors, and at other times, coordinators are assigned. There are both paid positions and volunteer positions in a children's ministry program. Regardless of the title or calling, remember to refresh yourself with Hosea 11:4, "I led them with cords of kindness, with the bands [or ties] of love." A congregation will reap great bins of blessings as they genuinely support, partner with, and trust their God-given Director of Children's Ministry.

Coping skills are important when working and dealing with volunteers. Coping skills help us to accept and get along with one another. Those skills enable us to welcome new ideas and to work together. They help us to be patient with one another. How to develop coping skills is an additional topic for a training meeting, especially when discussing conflict.

However, being flexible and able to cope are different from *tolerance*. Some things should not be tolerated, such as false doctrine or inappropriate behavior. At times, we may have to gently correct someone. Usually, one of two things will occur. Either they will become hurt and angry or they will repent and confess their error. Sometimes, confrontation is important for the sake of the Gospel.

If something in question does not contradict God's Word, does not take away from the goal, and does not hurt anyone or anything, you will need to determine if it is worth addressing. As the old adage goes, "Choose your battles wisely!" Now and then, it is better just to agree to disagree. That's acceptable as long as eternal salvation is not at stake. In the world of construction work, a head foreman may not be able to tolerate the irresponsible mistakes of a subcontractor for the sake of the future homeowner. He may have to fire or dismiss that careless worker. In children's ministry, we don't necessarily fire people. We may have to dismiss a volunteer, but only if a gentle, loving rebuke is unsuccessful and restoration is not possible. A Director of Children's Ministry or a Children's Ministry Leader is responsible for protecting the ministry and those involved, especially children, from any potentially spiritual or physical dangers.

Safety

The protection of children is a high priority in the church—not just from false doctrine, but also from physical danger. Be sure your child ministry volunteers are aware of and trained for the physical well-being of the children. Know the laws of your state regarding child protection. Have your board prepare a child protection policy about reporting possible child abuse. Discuss incorporating criminal background checks on volunteers. Have parents fill out a "Release of Liability, Indemnity Agreement, and Consent for Medical Treatment" form prepared by your church and approved by the church's insurance company.

Resource and prepare your team so they are ready in case there is a fire, storm, or even terrorist threats in the building. Watch for suspicious-looking individuals. Practice and discuss how to handle certain emergencies. Work out different scenarios and discuss them together. Be sure that all children's classrooms contain doors with a safety glass window to allow for visual observation as well as security.

Children also need to be protected from diseases. Have latex gloves available for diaper changes in the nursery. Make sure that toys are disinfected after each use. Be sure the children wash their hands before playing with play dough. Change the play dough often. Keep tissues and hand sanitizer close at hand. State clearly on a nursery wall poster about when not to leave children in the church child-care room, such as when they are sick, running a fever, or have a contagious rash. Keeping children safe and healthy is another way of showing Jesus' love.

Presentation

The word *transparency* seems to be finding its way into the church. How is that word defined? *Transparency* means "letting the light shine through." That is a great word to use if we are talking about letting others see Jesus in us. Another definition of transparency

is to be open, frank, and candid. If we use this second definition, caution must be practiced. The problem is that being open, frank, and candid could invite judgment and cause offense. On the other hand, honesty requires trust. God calls us to be honest and truthful with each other in a loving way, "speaking the truth in love" (Ephesians 4:15).

Now apply that to working with your TEAM of child ministry volunteers. How do you present yourself? Do you have good posture? Do you use appropriate words? Do you exhibit polite manners and respect for others? How you dress and present yourself can say volumes about who you are as a person. How will guests who visit your children's ministry events perceive your volunteers? How will you, as a leader, communicate these concerns to your volunteers or builders? How will you help your volunteers strive for excellence and not for the unattainable perfection?

How we present ourselves can make a difference. It can give security and confidence. It shows professionalism and genuine care. How the child ministry volunteers and leaders present themselves gives guests either a good or bad impression of the church. Through good presentation, God is honored. We reflect Jesus' light within us by what we say and do.

Obstacles

What comes to your mind when you hear the word *obstacle*? I think of heavy, giant glass bottles that are hard to get around or move. If you try to get them out of the way, they could fall over and break and cause even more problems. Obstacles are things that get in the way of something and prevent progress. They can take the form of many different things: time, objects, rules, lack of imagination, interruptions, inability, change, conflict, traditions, defiant will, pride, small spaces, lack of funds, and the list goes on. Wow! A lot of things can become an obstacle. Without a doubt, there will be obstacles in children's ministry.

When facing a frustration or conflict, it may help to look at it as an obstacle—something in the way that can be removed. There is hope. Take your obstacle to the foot of the cross. It may be a test, a trial, or an avenue to a new path God desires you to follow. Ask God for His power to help you overcome your obstacle. It may be in His plan to use it for His glory. Perhaps the obstacles you face will eventually bring glory to God. Maybe the obstacle will force you to become creative and work together with other volunteers for ideas, if funds are not available for a project your group wants to do. Perhaps further communication with another person will bring about understanding instead of competition. Thank God for your obstacle. When we are weak, we are strong, because then we rely on God instead of ourselves (2 Corinthians 12:10).

People's pasts, cultures, and personalities impact how they hear things, which can promote fear, stress, and fatigue and downright stop progress. Sometimes, leaders need to step back for a moment

With God-given faith, we can trust in Him to work all things for good and to give us wisdom in confronting our obstacles.

to better assess how to get around a certain obstacle. Should they creatively try to move it? How should they deal with the situation? An obstacle can feel like a huge mountain to move. Leaders may need to adjust accordingly. The Holy Spirit can help with that. He plants faith in us at our Baptism and gives us the power to lovingly communicate, teach, understand, forgive, and be patient. Jesus reminds His followers, "For truly, I say to you, if you have faith like a grain of mustard seed, you will say to this mountain, 'Move from here to there,' and it will move, and nothing will be impossible for you'" (Matthew 17:20). With God-given faith, we can trust in Him to work all things for good and to give us wisdom in confronting our obstacles.

Some obstacles come in the form of conflict. As the apostle Paul points out, we are all sinners (Romans 3:23). Therefore, it is beneficial to have personal peacekeeping and discipline plans in place. Unfortunately, conflict is inevitable. It is guaranteed. And it can bring ultimate disunity to your team. The storms of conflict may happen between director and volunteer, volunteer and volunteer, volunteer and parent, volunteer and child, parent and child, and so on. Do not be shocked when

REPRODUCIBLE BLUEPRINT

Turn to the back of the book to see the blueprint for personal peacemaking.

discords occur. Sometimes people are lured into a false sense of security believing that just because it is the *church* everyone will get along just fine, everything will be happy, and everyone will follow the group's shared ideas and plans. The opposite is actually true. No matter how well the plans are put in place, inevitably at some point something will not go as expected. Someone's feelings will get hurt, or some kind of misunderstanding will take place. Children's Ministry Blueprints that address reconciliation and discipline will help you to deal with conflicts and resolve them in a healthy and God-pleasing manner. The ideas given in the blueprint for discipline were inspired by a video from Christine Yount Jones, but I have made them my own. God's blessings as you adapt them for your own needs as well.

In California and other various parts of the country, builders often prepare the foundation of their buildings by making them earthquake-ready. It is an attempt to prevent damage from seismic activity. Many places across the country provide shelters in case of

REPRODUCIBLE BLUEPRINT

Turn to the back of the book to see the blueprint for discipline.

tornadoes or hurricanes. Conflict within the church can feel like some of these storms. And they can do a tremendous amount of damage. In fact, some are so devastating that the church must rebuild from the ground up to fix the damage. Children's Ministry Blueprints with a vision that anticipates these storms can be lifesaving.

Communication is imperative, especially during times of conflict or disagreement. Interestingly, builders use protective measures that are tried and true. They wear hard hats on the job site. They may wear safety glasses and gloves. They are careful where they walk and how they use their tools. When you encounter a disagreement or anticipate conflict, avoid communicating through email or text message. When discussing a difference of opinion or a potential disagreement, or even when trying to reconcile, make sure you do so in person, face-to-face. If that is impossible, then talk over the phone. Texts and emails are forms of communication that give people the opportunity to read between the lines. They can present your words in a different "voice" other than what you intended, which can create an even bigger conflict. Even the most well-written and loving emails have been taken the wrong way, allowing a situation to get completely out of hand. It is wise to use emails only for invitations, reminders, confirmations, registrations, or sharing some sort of resource. All other types of well-intended emails or text messages could end up backfiring!

Review your personal peacekeeping and discipline plans often with your child ministry volunteers. Bring it up in meetings. Try to do so before conflict arises, but also when conflict does occur. Communica-

Direct communication is imperative.

It is wise to only use emails for invitations, reminders, confirmations, registrations, or sharing some sort of resource.

tion and understanding are key. Listen to people, and listen to understand. Then, invite others to listen to you and one another. Talk often. Be patient with others and yourself. Stay positive and joyful in heart. Look for the good even in conflict. Keep a thankful attitude. The Holy Spirit can help you; ask Him. Every person has been bought with a price—the blood of Jesus (1 Corinthians 6:20; Matthew 13:45–46). Martin Luther reminds us in the Eighth Commandment to put the best construction on everything. Remember that Satan is the enemy—not God's people.

In many ways, conflict can actually bring people closer together once forgiveness and restoration has taken place. So, don't be afraid of conflict. God can use conflict for His purposes, and He does! Look at the story of Joseph and his brothers. Jacob's sons were jealous of their brother Joseph. At first, they threw him in a pit and then sold him as a slave. The envious brothers sent Joseph's coat that they had stained with goat's blood to their father, leading him to believe that a fierce animal had devoured his beloved son. Later, Joseph found favor in the eyes of the Pharaoh and became second-in-command of all of Egypt. There was a famine in the land and Joseph's brothers traveled to Egypt to purchase grain. They failed to recognize their brother Joseph, to whom they had been so cruel, but Joseph recognized them. Eventually, he informed them of his identity, embraced them, and willingly forgave them. He told his brothers that God had used their evil act for good and to preserve life. His brothers wept. Their long-fractured relationship was healed, and their lives were saved. (See Genesis 45:3–8.)

Builders working together are often confronted

with fears. They need lots of encouragement. Expectations and disappointments can pounce before anyone knows what hit them. Support and understanding are needed. Conditions of body and mind can limit and weaken builders. They need someone to come alongside and help them to accomplish what they hope to achieve. Live in the promises of God, knowing He loves you and has power and control over all things. Jesus forgives us when we fail Him and one another. Let us, too, be quick and generous with forgiveness. Building relationships builds a ministry. And forgiveness cements everything together!

Blueprints for Your Own Blueprints

How are Children's Ministry Blueprints created?

When preparing a children's ministry manual for your church, consider calling it (Name of your church)'s Blueprints for Children's Ministry. Calling it "blueprints" instead of a "manual" gives the perception that these are more like friendly guidelines and can be altered as time goes on and as the need arises. A manual is a booklet giving information or instructions. Since it is a term that has been used for many years, it can give the impression that your manual is some kind of a sacred "law book" that the church has established. Everyone had better adhere to it—or else! Using the term *manual*, no one would ever think of questioning it or revising it. When people hear the word *manual*, they tend to think management. And that has the potential of becoming so important to people that they consider it "hands off" or nonnegotiable. Yet, it generally has no bearing upon or basis from Scripture. It is neither right nor wrong. It is mostly tradition. To avoid this unnecessary conflict, make sure that these blueprints are shared in a way that adaptations and improvements are welcome.

REPRODUCIBLE BLUEPRINT

To get started and review blueprints for your own children's ministry, turn to the back of this book for many examples!

The structure for the second portion of *Blueprints for Children's Ministry* will provide a path or a guideline to follow and will help you keep focused. Let's clarify some terms and get started. A goal, a purpose, an objective, and an activity are used to create guidelines. They are helpful in knowing *what* (goal), *why* (purpose), and *how* (objective) you are to build.

GOAL: A long-term aim that gives focus. It is *what* you want to achieve and where you want to end up. *Example:* Build a house.

PURPOSE: The reason *why* you want to get to the goal. It also gives motivation to reach the goal. *Example:* To provide shelter for a family to live.

*Include Scripture passages here if writing for an overall ministry. It's the anchor for the "why."

OBJECTIVE: *How* to achieve the goal. *Example:* Design, plan, and implement.

ACTIVITY: Directed, detailed, and specific efforts to fulfill the objective. *Example:* Tools, workers, supplies, and so on.

REFLECTION: The evaluation of how well the goal and objectives are being met and whether the activities need to be adjusted. This sometimes is referred to as an assessment. Using the softer word *reflection* helps remove the management of the action and keeps the mode of leadership and teamwork. *Example:* The new saw worked well. And maybe we could try pneumatic hammers next time to get the job done faster.

Questionnaires . . .
"Did we reach our goal?"
or "Was our objective
achieved?"

REPRODUCIBLE BLUEPRINT

To get started and review blueprints for your own children's ministry, turn to the back of this book for many examples!

own. Adopt them just as they are or revise, re-create, and expand on them. Make new ones, if necessary. The following samples are offered to help get you started. Use them as a resource for your own unique set of blueprints for your church.

Certain blueprints may seem apparent to some people, such as children's offering. However, upon reviewing the goal, purpose, and objective of the offering, it will become more dynamic and significant than previously thought. If volunteers see the importance in something, they will in turn be able to communicate that to the children and their parents. People will not attend or participate in something unless they see the value in it.

Numerous books and resources are available to help with other topics and details of children's ministry. The goal of this book is to be a time-saving how-to resource. It is designed to assist churches as they begin and implement their children's ministry. It will also help to expand, evaluate, and clarify their existing children's ministry program. Perhaps it will even give some insight and inspiration for the sake of the Church and her little souls. It should be kept readily accessible for the purpose of creating new blueprints. Use it as a starter for whatever children's ministry adventure you are ready to explore in a children's ministry meeting. A lot of work, thought, and time is required to create blueprints. Take your time. Make as many revised versions as needed until you and your team come up with a blueprint that is just right for your congregation. Remember to pray throughout the whole creative process that the Lord

When providing a questionnaire for volunteers to give feedback on a particular event, include questions that can be used as a teaching tool for the volunteers. "Did we reach our goal?" or "Was our objective achieved?" These types of questions help volunteers keep goals and objectives in mind when they participate in the next planned event. If we only stay focused on the activities without keeping the goal and objectives in mind, we will most likely miss the purpose.

Keep your blueprints in line with Scripture, as well as your church's mission and vision. At the end of this chapter are sample blueprints for children's ministry. You can either adopt or adapt them as you write your is at the heart of your construction project.

Blueprints are useful for all areas of ministry. The Board of Christian Education, the Preschool Board, the Day School Board, the Board of Children's Ministry, the Board of Youth Ministry, and so forth can all benefit from their own set of blueprints. Even if your congregation does not have boards and uses a less structured means of ministry, blueprints are still essential. Blueprints are plans, actions, policies, strategies, directions, and structure. Use as few words as possible to be understandable and clear. State only the necessary information. People are overloaded in life and face many time constraints. If instructions are too verbose, few people will take the time to read the blueprints.

There are occasions when writing that it is okay to keep language simple even if it is not always grammatically correct. A great example of this would be the language used in the original 1957 *Little Visits with God*, a children's devotional book through Concordia Publishing House. The authors were concerned for the child, and therefore used popular even though sometimes "incorrect" grammar and simplified some of the Bible verses. There may be times when this type of simplicity is needed while writing blueprints. A blueprint example of this would be when listing things with bullet points for a job or ministry description. Use simple creative privilege to use as few words as possible.

Every situation is different for each congregation. If you are a congregation with an existing children's ministry program, be careful not to implement change to your current practices and programs just for the sake of change. This usually does not lead to a good outcome. Make sure you have a good reason for the change. Always keep your goal, purpose, and objectives in mind when considering new ideas. Sometimes it is helpful to use the word *add* instead of *change* if something new is being introduced. *Add* is a softer word and puts a positive spin on things. It can ignite excitement in those who fear change. Fre-

quently, change is not what upsets people. Rather, it is the emotion of a "loss" that generally causes resistance to change.

The remaining pages, after this chapter, are ready-made sample blueprints. Congregations can use these as a starting point in creating their own. Some of the events listed may not be applicable to your situation. There may be other events not listed that you will want to create and add to your Children's Ministry Blueprints. Read, use, and build upon these blueprints as the Lord leads and guides you to serve His children and equip His children to serve.

Remember to review and revise your own blueprints frequently. Add to them as your children's ministry grows. Do not leave your blueprints on the shelf; keep them handy. Use them as active instruments. Pray often for the children and parents of your congregation. Pray privately, as well as with your child ministry team.

Blueprints can contain many opportunities for people to serve in child ministry positions. Perhaps your congregation is small, and you think that your children's ministry will be shorthanded. It has been said that in any typical congregation only 20 percent of the members do 80 percent of the work. I don't know for sure if that is true. However, if so, I wonder if that happens because we forget to personally ask people to help. Or when we do ask for help, we fail to explain clearly what their responsibilities would all entail. Perhaps we also fail to establish good relationships with people. Do we know what spiritual gifts and talents they possess? What needs match their ability to accomplish the task? Sometimes, we only focus on the outcome of a goal rather than the process. In doing so, we lose people along the way. Some ministry responsibilities can be combined, depending on the number of available people able to serve. When blueprints are shared, combined with much prayer, you will be delightfully surprised at how much any size church can do. People will become excited to help once relationships are built. Trust our gracious

Lord. He will never let you down.

Some congregations provide a preschool or an elementary day school as part of their ministry. The leadership of a healthy children's ministry program can help to bridge the gap between the school and the church. This results in fantastic benefits and blessings for both the congregation and the school. By offering the children's ministry program to the day school and preschool children, it will give them further opportunities to learn about God and take part in Christian fellowship. Children participating in these events receive many open doors for faith nurture, service, and friendship. They will benefit from church involvement through the building of solid Christian relationships. Consequently, there will be congregational support for the school and vice versa. Congregational members, child ministry volunteers, and pastors who are involved and visible at the school can conduct outreach and evangelism. A strong relationship between the church and school will result in less competition and more cooperation. Together, they can focus on the Great Commission. It also relays the message that the children of the school and their families are important to the church and that God loves them very much. Develop blueprints to show what that bridge and relationship will look like in your church.

Remember to include in your blueprints a child protection plan, policies for background checks on volunteers, a release of liability, an indemnity agreement, consent for medical treatment forms, and reconciliation procedures. These are all a part of and essential to the frame-

REPRODUCIBLE BLUEPRINT
To get started and review blueprints for your own children's ministry, turn to the back of this book for many examples!

work for the building to stand strong. They, too, may need revising and updating over time.

Each congregation is unique in its own way. Its personality, culture, needs, number of children, building size, finances, and resources are different from every other church. For that reason, there is no right or wrong set of blueprints as long as God's Word is upheld. The foundation, God's Word, and the cornerstone, Christ Jesus, are the same for every congregation. God calls His Church to provide discipleship for people of all ages. How this is carried out and built upon is as individual as each congregation. Just remember that children's ministry all begins at birth.

May God bless you and give you courage as you bravely construct your child ministry and trustingly fabricate your children's ministry program. Blessings as you follow God, *the* Almighty Architect! Gladly embrace His lead. Keep building to the glory of God!

Isn't it strange that Princes and Kings
And Clowns that caper in Sawdust Rings
And ordinary folk like you and me
Are builders of eternity . . .

To each is given a bag of tools
An hour glass and a book of rules
And each must build ere his time has flown
A stumbling block or a stepping stone.

—*R. Lee Sharpe*

BLUEPRINTS FOR YOUR CHILDREN'S MINISTRY
Table of Contents

The remaining pages are ready-made sample blueprints. Use these as a starting point in creating your own "Children's Ministry Blueprints." Some of the events listed may not be applicable to your situation. There may be other events not listed that you will want to create and add to your Children's Ministry Blueprints. Read, use, and build upon these blueprints as the Lord leads and guides you to equip His children to serve.

The Children's Ministry

_____
(Church name)

_____
(City and state)

Goal (Chief aim)

Children will continue to grow in faith and in their personal relationships with Jesus Christ.

Purpose (The reason why you want to get to your goal)

- To fulfill God's command to let the little children come to Him (Matthew 19:13–15)

- To recognize the children's examples of faith (Mark 10:15)

- To give children opportunities to express their faith (Matthew 18:2–5)

Objectives (What you want to accomplish)

- Help parents introduce Jesus' love to their child from birth.

- Give children knowledge and understanding of God's Word.

- Lead children in worship involvement suited to their level of ability and expression of their Christian faith through joyful praise.

- Guide children in sharing, mission activity, and stewardship in the Christian life.

- Offer children opportunities for Christian fellowship and to witness their faith.

- Provide experiences for children to build Christian character and put their love for God into action.

Activities (This is where you list all the details that will help accomplish the objective)

- Cradle roll
- Cradle roll banner
- Cradle cooks
- Little Ones' Quiet Room
- Basket of Blessings or worship bags
    - Children's worship bulletins
    - Treats for Toddlers
- Tender Care Nursery
- Little Lambs and Ewe—Mom and Me Playgroup
- Sunday School
    - Bible lessons and creative activities to reinforce lessons
    - Bible Words to Remember
    - Offerings
    - Music/Praise
    - Prayer
- Christian education Sunday/rally day
    - Special worship participation
    - Picnic
- Children's helping opportunities at church
- TEAM 56 (Grades 5 and 6)
    - Acolyte
    - First Communion class
- Children's choirs
- Liturgical dance
- Kids' Night Out—Bible Blast!

REPRODUCIBLE
BLUEPRINT

- Puppet ministry
- Parenting classes
- Fall Harvest Fellowship
- Family Christmas worship service
- Hearts for Jesus
- Children's Lenten Art Show
- New Life Festival
- Vacation Bible School
- Children's ministry directory

Mission (What the church is called by God to do)

We will serve the children of the church by joyfully sharing God's love and His Word with them while providing opportunities for their ministry in order to help parents build lifelong disciples.

Vision
(What the mission will look like)

- Relationships with parents, children, and child ministry volunteers
- Opportunities for children to learn about and follow Jesus
- Available resources for parents to raise their children in the faith
- Training, guidance, and support for children's ministry volunteers
- Congregational responsibility and support through the appointing and encouraging of leaders, the building and maintaining of programs, financial backing, and prayer

Tagline (a catch phrase so people will easily remember the mission and vision/an easy identification)

"Feeding His Lambs to Shine His Light"

Director of Children's Ministry

Job Description

Goal

He or she will develop, organize, implement, and maintain the children's ministry at (name of congregation).

Purpose

The qualified director will work with and under the pastor in order to actively maintain the faith nurturing and ministry of God's children in the congregation.

Objectives

- Cast the vision of the children's ministry program.
- Train child ministry volunteers.
- Partner with parents in faith development of their children.
- Implement the Blueprints for Children's Ministry.
- Monitor and secure the mission and vision of the children's ministry.

Qualifications and Spiritual Gifts

- A member of the congregation who is faithful in worship, Bible study, and prayer
- Has a college degree and educational background in child and faith development
- In agreement with the church's theological beliefs
- Knowledge in Christian educational administration
- Seeks guidance from the Holy Spirit
- A passion for faith development in children
- Experience in working with children

- Able to work well and communicate with people
- Leadership and organizational skills
- Creative minded
- Encourager
- Compassionate
- Enthusiastic
- Visionary

Specific Responsibilities

1. Recruit, train, equip, supervise, support, and encourage child ministry volunteers and coordinators for children's ministry that covers children in the congregation from birth through the sixth grade.

2. Help assume the responsibility of any children's ministry activity if a volunteer child ministry worker vacancy occurs.

3. Evaluate, select, develop, and implement curriculum for children's ministry, paying careful attention to doctrine and seeking curriculum approval of the pastor.

4. Order curriculum and other resources as needed, or delegate others to use the church federal tax ID number to purchase approved resources.

5. Obtain periodicals and other resources for enrichment and make them available to child ministry workers.

6. Encourage and promote child ministry volunteers to participate in children's ministry-related workshops and training events.

7. Maintain a master calendar for children's ministry activities scheduled in accordance with the church master calendar.

8. Attend church staff meetings.

9. Work with child ministry volunteers, encouraging and enabling them to develop good communication and relationships with the children's parents, develop relationships with the children, and encourage child ministry volunteers to help the children build relationships with other children in the church.

10. Implement the Blueprints for Children's Ministry, and yearly create a children's ministry directory.

11. Communicate children's ministry "news" to the congregation through Sunday worship folder (bulletin), the church newsletter, appropriate bulletin boards, and technological means available.

12. Develop, promote, and implement outreach and in-reach opportunities in children's ministry.

13. Maintain accurate records and updated files of the children's ministry for future reference and assessment.

14. Develop and manage a budget for children's ministry using good stewardship of the funds.

15. Keep in open communication with the senior pastor for guidance, for evaluating the effectiveness of this ministry and its programming, and for mutual encouragement in uplifting the saints.

16. Assist the pastor with preschool and day school chapels when needed.

17. Be visible at the preschool and day school to welcome the children and their parents, attend various preschool and day school events, and provide invitations to children's ministry opportunities. Be available to help with preschool and day school emergencies or vital last-minute needs should they arise.

18. Implement safety precautions such as outlet plugs, evacuation maps, first-aid kits, choking and resuscitation demonstration posters, and any other helpful safety measures.

19. Ex officio on the Board of Children's Ministry and work with the board that is responsible for hiring workers in the church to employ qualified nursery attendants (babysitters). Inform that same board, if the time comes, that a child-care provider is no longer capable and should be dismissed. Keep a running schedule for the nursery attendant. See to it that the nursery and quiet room are safe, functional, and maintained. Train and equip the child-care providers (nursery attendants and babysitters). Maintain the pagers, pager binder, sign-in sheet, and supplies required.

20. Develop good relationships with the parents of the children in the congregation. Provide opportunities to equip parents in teaching their children about God, offer encouragement, and help them to connect with the church and other member families.

21. Recognize the birthday and Baptism birthday of children in the congregation.

22. Keep the children of the congregation, their parents, and the child ministry volunteers in prayer.

Reports to the senior pastor. The congregational hiring board determines hours of work and salary.

Safety Guidelines for Child Ministry

_____

(Church name)

Classroom Environment:

- Arrive at least 5–10 minutes prior to a program or event and check for the cleanliness of chairs, tables, and so on.
- Cover any exposed outlets.
- Pick up objects that children could fall over or onto.
- Make adjustments if the room is too warm or too cold.
- Make sure old garbage has been removed so bad odors do not exist.
- When using a candle or flame for a project or devotion, first alert the Director of Children's Ministry or other leader. Use artificial flame whenever possible. Always remember to follow fire-safety rules and extinguish candles after use. Any flame is prohibited in the nursery.
- Obtain and use tissues and nonalcoholic hand sanitizer when needed.
- Make sure fans are out of reach of children's fingers.
- If you open a window, make sure to close and lock it before you leave.
- Return the thermostat to its previous setting.
- If you unlocked a door, lock it before you leave, or find a responsible person to make sure it is locked before he or she leaves.

Child Care:

- Loving hugs are encouraged.
- Never touch children in inappropriate ways, such as in areas where a swimming suit would cover.
- Never grab, push, or pull children in anger.
- Never leave children alone.
- Do not take children off campus without the knowledge and consent of the Director of Children's Ministry or other leader and written consent of guardians.
- Children are to remain in the building unless knowledge and consent of Director of Children's Ministry or other leader is obtained or there is an emergency.
- Do not allow children to go to the restroom alone. An adult or designated assistant should take small children, but older children can go with a buddy. Whoever goes with the child should also allow for privacy.
- Make sure that when a program or event is over, children are reconnected to their parents or guardians.

In case of fire or other reason for evacuation:

- Stay calm.
- Follow evacuation map on room walls. If that is not available, lead the children out the closest possible exit and gather in one area outside, away from danger.
- Make sure all children in your care are present. Count them.
- Reenter the building only when there is no longer any danger.

Personal Peacemaking

"Blessed are the peacemakers, for they shall be called sons of God."

Matthew 5:9

Because of the peace that God won for us through His Son, Jesus Christ, we, too, want to respond and are called to be peacemakers.

Scripture informs us that we are all sinners and daily fall short of the glory of God (Romans 3:23). Working as a team in children's ministry, we know that there are going to be times when conflict will arise—whether over misunderstandings; hurt feelings; differences in values, goals, expectations, interests, or opinions; competition over limited resources; sinful attitudes and desires; or sinful words and actions.

Our Lord Jesus has taught us what to do when someone sins against us. He says in Matthew 18:

"If your brother sins against you, go and tell him his fault, between you and him alone. If he listens to you, you have gained your brother. But if he does not listen, take one or two others along with you, that every charge may be established by the evidence of two or three witnesses. If he refuses to listen to them, tell it to the church. And if he refuses to listen even to the church, let him be to you as a Gentile and a tax collector." (vv. 15–17)

Notice, the first thing we are to do is to go only to the person who has sinned against us. We are not to go around and gossip about it to others. Go straight to the person with whom we are in conflict. If we don't, the situation will only get worse. We are to try to restore the broken relationship. God would have us to do everything possible to protect not only our own reputation, but especially the reputation of the one who has sinned against us. It is the loving, Christlike thing to do. That is

why Martin Luther writes about it in his meaning of the Eighth Commandment:

"You shall not give false testimony against your neighbor. *What does this mean?* We should fear and love God so that we do not tell lies about our neighbor, betray him, slander him, or hurt his reputation, but defend him, speak well of him, and explain everything in the kindest way." (Eighth Commandment and its meaning)

The following are some helpful reminders when we do run into conflict:

- Our goal is to glorify God in all that we do and give witness to what Christ has done for us in every situation.

"So, whether you eat or drink, or whatever you do, do all to the glory of God." (1 Corinthians 10:31)

- We begin the peacemaking process by getting the log out of our own eye. Take time to think about how we may have contributed to the conflict and what we need to do to help resolve it.

"Judge not, that you be not judged. For with

REPRODUCIBLE BLUEPRINT

the judgment you pronounce you will be judged, and with the measure you use it will be measured to you. Why do you see the speck that is in your brother's eye, but do not notice the log that is in your own eye? Or how can you say to your brother, 'Let me take the speck out of your eye,' when there is the log in your own eye? You hypocrite, first take the log out of your own eye, and then you will see clearly to take the speck out of your brother's eye." (Matthew 7:1–5)

- Next we will want to gently restore. How can we humbly help others to understand how they have contributed to the conflict so that we can heal the broken relationship?

"Brothers, if anyone is caught in any transgression, you who are spiritual should restore him in a spirit of gentleness. Keep watch on yourself, lest you too be tempted. Bear one another's burdens, and so fulfill the law of Christ. For if anyone thinks he is something, when he is nothing, he deceives himself. But let each one test his own work, and then his reason to boast will be in himself alone and not in his neighbor. For each will have to bear his own load." (Galatians 6:1–5)

- Then we want to go and be reconciled. We want to demonstrate forgiveness and encourage a reasonable solution to the conflict.

"Then Peter came up and said to Him, 'Lord, how often will my brother sin against me, and I forgive him? As many as seven times?' Jesus said to him, 'I do not say to you seven times, but seventy-seven times.'" (Matthew 18:21–22)

In the Bible study *Blessed Are the Peacemakers*, we also find the following helpful information.

Personal Peacemaking Responses

There are three biblical ways to resolve conflicts personally and privately, just between you and the other party:

- **Overlook an Offense**—Many disputes are so

insignificant that they should be resolved by quietly overlooking an offense (Proverbs 19:11). "Overlooking" biblically, means forgiving without talking to the other person.

- **Reconciliation**—If an offense is too serious to overlook or has damaged the relationship, we need to reconcile personal or relational issues through confession, loving correction, and forgiveness (see Matthew 5:23–24; 18:15; Galatians 6:1; Colossians 3:13).

- **Negotiation**—Even if we successfully reconcile relational issues, we may still need to work through material issues related to money, property, or other rights (Philippians 2:3–4).

Through all of this, remember that God's response to contrition (sorrow for sin) and faith is forgiveness of sins through His Son, Jesus Christ. God proclaims this good news of His forgiveness to both new believers and experienced believers.

Forgive and restore the repentant.

Whenever someone is moved to repent, the sinner must be immediately comforted with the good news of God's forgiveness. If you hear someone else's confession, do not leave him in his guilt. Share God's gift of mercy with him. It can be as simple as reading one of the many Scriptures that proclaim God's forgiveness. To help the sinner understand how personally our God grants us His gift, insert his name in the appropriate place in the verse. Scripture is a powerful Means of Grace that comforts us and empowers us to live as the children of God.

Our job is to speak the truth in love as clearly and persuasively as possible. God's job is to change people's hearts.

Excerpts from *Blessed Are the Peacemakers* © 2004 by Ambassadors of Reconciliation, pages 11, 12, and 26.

Discipline

_____
(Church name)

Scripture holds within its pages a blueprint for discipline:

"And we urge you, brothers, admonish the idle, encourage the fainthearted, help the weak, be patient with them all." (I Thessalonians 5:14)

First of all, discern why the child is misbehaving. Determine if the child is **idle** (*defiant*), **fainthearted** (*emotional*), or **weak** (*unable*).

When a child is **idle**, lazy, hard-nosed, hardhearted, or unruly, Scripture says to warn that person. There needs to be firm admonition toward him or her. That type of behavior needs consequences to be explained followed by choices. Be sure to follow through on those choices given and the results promised. Use sentences such as, "When you do (*this*), then (*this*) or (*this*) will happen" and "These are your choices . . ." There needs to be both a *consequence* and a *choice* for the idle child. Respond more firmly when their behavior is out of defiant rebellion.

When a child is **fainthearted**, timid, shy, nervous, hesitant, or afraid, deal with him or her more tenderly and offer encouragement. With this type of child, do not use *strong* words, such as, "You do (*this*) and you are going to be in time-out—you have a choice." Instead, use *softer* words, such as, "What's going on? Why don't you want to join in? Please help me understand." You want to find out how and why they are feeling a certain way and deal with them on an emotional level of understanding. For example, if the child is supposed to run in a game and they are afraid of falling down, you can use words like, "I'll run with you and help you!" Come alongside them and give them encouragement, confidence, and support. Ask yourself, "How can I talk children through their feelings, or are they disobeying because they feel they are not competent? How can I help them to feel competent?"

When a child is **weak**, give compassionate and sensitive care to him or her. Some children just don't have the skills needed for what they are asked to do, or they may be tired, not strong enough, or physically challenged. Equip them for the task at hand. They may not know what to do. Use words like, "Let me help you. I can show you how to do this. I will come alongside you. We can work together. Let's be partners." If children don't know how to do something, they may be embarrassed. Perhaps they can't see because they are sitting too far away, or they can't hear what is going on, so they lose interest. Perhaps they feel inadequate doing something, so they just act up. Help them.

Finally, Scripture advises us to be enduring, long-suffering, accommodating, cooperative, merciful, compassionate, supportive, kind, accepting, gracious, forgiving, uncomplaining, helpful, and just downright patient with one another. That models God's love and helps children to be a healthy part of the group or classroom and grow in their relationships with Jesus and others.

Children's Helping Opportunities at Church

_____
(Church name)

Goal

The children will serve God and minister to others by helping at church and church-related events.

Purpose

- Children at an early age will experience and express their natural joy in being helpful.

- Children will be enriched in a sense of belonging and being needed in the church family.

- Children will develop awareness of ways they can show love to God and their church family by caring for His house and those who worship there.

Objectives

- Child ministry volunteers will be aware of opportunities where children can be helpful at church and offer and assign age-appropriate tasks.

- Parents will be informed of the purpose of children being helpful at church and will encourage their children to do so.

Activities

- Toddlers will help take care of God's house by returning items used from the Basket of Blessings and throw their empty treat bags in the garbage after worship.

- During snack time, the Parents and Twos Sunday School class children will be appointed to take turns handing out cups and napkins and will "feed Mr. Garbage Can" their trash after snack time is over.

- Children will serve as "child ushers" by handing out children's bulletins to other children before worship services. It serves better if teens or adults, in a church worship service, gather the offering from the congregation. Children can help collect offerings during the Sunday School hour from their fellow classmates. Determine at what age the children begin to acolyte. Letters are sent to parents explaining about this activity.

- On cleanup day at church, the children will help wash and dry the toys from the nursery and clean tables and chairs from their Sunday School rooms.

- At church picnics or potluck meals, the children will help set out utensils, napkins, and cups. Older children can help parents and other adults and teens set up chairs and tables and help take them down again after the meal is over.

- The altar guild can hold a special meeting where they show children the care they do for God's house and what the children can do themselves to care for the church sanctuary (dusting, sharpening pew pencils, picking up litter, caring for the hymnals, and the like).

- During Sunday School, VBS, or other child gathering events, child ministry volunteers will look for opportunities for giving the children an occasion to serve others by helping.

List more activities as opportunities, situations, and events arise.

Reflection

Are the child ministry volunteers adequately trained on how to assist children with the opportunities to help? Have the parents been informed about the purpose of their children helping at church? How are the children developing through this process?

Children's Ministry Building Blocks for Christian Character

(Church name)

Believers are transformed people, filled with the Holy Spirit through hearing the Word and in the waters of Baptism. Living out these new lives, we serve one another with freedom and joy! Children's ministry recognizes that children who follow Jesus will honor and pursue biblical instruction with the help of the Holy Spirit living in them. Therefore, these building blocks are presented as ways for children to implement God-pleasing attitudes and behaviors as their personalities develop and as they grow as children of God. With the help of the Holy Spirit, their Christian character is formed as followers of Christ to shine His light. "Let no one despise you for your youth, but set the believers an example in speech, in conduct, in love, in faith, in purity" (1 Timothy 4:12).

Help children not to focus on what they must do, but instead on what Jesus did for us. He lived the perfect life we cannot live, and He washed away our sins when we fail to live our lives in love. It is now He who lives inside us (Galatians 2:20) since our Baptism. With Jesus' Spirit living in us, we can trust Him to help us follow His instructions. Because of that, "I can do all things through Him who strengths me" (Philippians 4:13). When children are shown that it is God who gives them the ability to obey and follow, they will learn to give God the glory for everything they do. Remind children to ask Jesus for His help and that they can trust that He will always help them.

To God:

With Jesus living in me,

- He will help me seek to honor the Lord in all that I think, say, and do (Deuteronomy 26:17).
- The Holy Spirit helps me to recognize the Scriptures as the final source of truth, and He will help me to submit myself to their authority (2 Timothy 3:16–17).
- He will help me remember that my behavior and appearance reflect not only on me but also on Him (1 Corinthians 10:31).

- I have a humble and repentant attitude, which leads me to ask forgiveness when I sin (1 John 1:8–9).

To my parents:

Jesus will help me to

- honor my parents in everything I think, say, and do (Exodus 20:12).
- seek to learn all that I can from them (Psalm 78:1–8).
- obey them in the Lord (Ephesians 6:1–3).

To my church:

Jesus will help me to

- love my church and submit to the governing authorities (Romans 13:1–6; Titus 2).
- make worship and spiritual growth a priority in my life (Psalm 95:1–7; John 4:23–24; Romans 12:1–2).
- be an ambassador for Him wherever I am (Matthew 28:18–20).

To my teachers:

Jesus will help me to

- demonstrate respect, attentiveness, gratitude, and obedience to my teachers (Hebrews 13:17).

- do the work I have been assigned with diligence and integrity (Ephesians 5:8–17).
- do my best to learn and achieve (Philippians 4:8–9).

To my classmates:

Jesus will help me to

- honor and respect the time, work, and feelings of other children (Romans 12:9–18).
- model honesty, integrity, kindness, and modesty in my relationships (Galatians 5:22–25; Philippians 2:3–7).
- strive for peace in everything I do (Ephesians 4:1–6).

(The list above is adapted from materials developed with the collaboration of Pastor Herb Mirley and Dr. Bill Kamm and are referenced here with permission.)

Incorporating optional activities:

- This makes for a great children's Bible study. Stress that we can do nothing on our own, but it is Jesus who loves to help us. Include praising prayers that He is our great God who helps us, I'm-sorry prayers for forgiveness when we forget to rely on His help, asking prayers for Jesus to help, trusting prayers to confess faith that He will help us, and thanking prayers for His help.
- Use parts each Sunday to include in a Sunday School class or Sunday School openings or closings.
- Apply this to a Christian school, or teach a simplified version in a Christian preschool.
- Create a poster using these character standards for use at church or Christian Day School classrooms, or encourage children to hang this in a special place at home.

Partnering with Parents

_____
(Church name)

Goal

Our congregation will connect with parents.

Purpose

To support parents in their responsibility of nurturing their children in the faith (Deuteronomy 6:4–9)

Objective

Our congregation will develop a personal relationship with parents in the church and inform, resource, encourage, and communicate with them.

Activities

- Cradle cook meals for families with a newborn baby.
- Cradle roll mailing.
- Let the parents get to know who you are and how you and the church care for their family.
- Home visits.
- Phone calls.
- Informational letters updating parents as to what their child is being taught.
- Invitations on upcoming children's ministry activities.
- A warm hello at church and conversation to build a relationship of care and interest.
- Offer and advertise parenting classes that teach about age-related stages of child development, Christian discipline, and spiritual concept levels in children.
- Newsletter and bulletin articles that provide ideas for parents on how to teach their children church manners, how to help their child focus and follow along in worship, balancing Law and Gospel in the home in regards to Ephesians 6:4.
- Provide information about Sunday School and other faith-growth opportunities.
- Offer opportunities for parents to encourage their children to worship, help, serve, give, and witness their faith.
- Encourage family devotions at home: set up example child devotional books or hold workshop.
- Give examples for families to write out their family goals.
- Involve "empty nesters" and the older generations in needed areas of help with young families.
- Give reminders to parents about their child's baptismal birthday and ways to celebrate.
- Make available faith-nurturing resources, such as children's religious books, children's Bibles, children's religious music CDs (church library and book orders).
- Provide information about adult Bible studies and encourage parents to be in God's Word.
- Recommend Christian books that are helpful guides to the young child's faith development.
- Provide children's worship bulletins to enhance children's worship experience with their family.

Reflection

How are the relationships developing? What else could be done to further relationships with the parents? Are parents receptive toward working together and receiving helpful information? Which parents could use more one-on-one conversations or a listening ear? Are the needs of the parents being met with the resources being offered? What other recourses or classes could be offered? Are all parents aware of the church nursery, quiet room, and how their child can check out a church library book?

Cradle Ministry Coordinator

Ministry Description

_____

(Church name)

1. A member of the church who is committed to faithful worship, Bible study, and prayer, and communicates well with others.

2. Works closely with the Director of Children's Ministry in assessing the activities and overseeing and encouraging those who carry out the responsibilities of

    - Cradle roll (Cradle Roll Representative),
    - Cradle roll banner (Cradle Roll Banner Crafter), and
    - Cradle cooks (Cradle Cook Head).

3. Work closely with and consult with the Director of Children's Ministry to maintain the quiet room, Basket of Blessings, and worship bags to remain

    - clean,
    - safe,
    - orderly, and
    - stocked.

4. Obtain resources from the Director of Children's Ministry.

REPRODUCIBLE
BLUEPRINT

Blueprints for Children's Ministry © 2017 Concordia Publishing House. Reproduced by permission for church use.

Cradle Roll

_____
(Church name)

Goal

Register congregational infants and toddlers and implement cradle roll packets.

Purpose

- Parents receive guidance of ways to introduce Jesus' love to their children from birth and support for their children's spiritual well-being.

- The church demonstrates to parents that the church cares for them and their little ones.

- Detailed record-keeping for future purposes, such as knowing when to celebrate the children's birthdays and baptismal days and when to invite and enroll the children in Sunday School.

Objective

Parents of newborns through age 3 are provided with materials that include the nurturing of their children's spiritual, emotional, and physical development, while at the same time birth and baptismal dates are recorded of member children.

Activities

- The Director of Children's Ministry (DCM) will order cradle roll (or nursery roll) packets from a religious publishing house for the cradle roll representative to give to parents.

- As soon as there is a new baby born in the congregation, the church office will contact the DCM who will then contact the cradle roll representative.

- Cradle roll materials will be mailed out on a scheduled basis by the cradle roll representative.

- To begin building a relationship with both newborn and family, the Cradle Ministry Coordinator or other representative could make a visit to the family and present the first mailing. Always call ahead first to make sure the family is comfortable with this welcome.

Reflection

Are the materials being sent out in a timely manner to the correct address? Is the information about the newborn getting to the cradle roll representative in a timely manner? Are the cradle roll materials that are being used updated? Are ALL the eligible children who are members of the congregation included on the cradle roll roster?

REPRODUCIBLE BLUEPRINT

Cradle Roll Representative

Ministry Description

_____
(Church name)

1. Receive approved cradle roll packets from Director of Children's Ministry for new parents.

2. Represent the child ministry of the congregation by welcoming, encouraging, and supporting new parents through the cradle roll mailings and other opportunities, such as phone calls, contacts at church, and personal visits, when possible.

3. Mail out cradle roll (or nursery roll) materials in a timely manner.

4. Maintain the cradle roll packets and keeps them organized.

5. Notify the Director of Children's Ministry when more cradle roll packets need to be ordered.

6. Present postage receipts to Director of Children's Ministry for reimbursement.

7. When a family transfers to another congregation and their child is still on the cradle roll, give the family the rest of the cradle roll packet to take with them, or send the remaining packet to the new congregation.

8. If a new family with a child under age 3 joins the congregation or transfers in from another church, start them on a cradle roll packet using the appropriate age materials and place unused materials from the packet in a folder to be used if needed for other children at another time.

REPRODUCIBLE
BLUEPRINT

Cradle Roll Banner

_____
(Church name)

Goal

The church will hang a banner displaying the names of the children in the cradle roll of the church.

Purpose

Observing a cradle roll banner, parents and their young children will recognize that their church cherishes them; loves, cares for, and values them; and considers them a part of the church family.

Objective

Create a banner that visually acknowledges children of the church from birth to age 3, including their name, birth date, and baptismal date.

Activities

- The banner, which includes newborn babies' names and birth dates, would be hung in a place where parents of babies and young children would see it often (possibly the quiet room or nursery).
- Baby's baptismal date will be added after the Baptism.
- The Director of Children's Ministry will let the Cradle Roll Banner Crafter know new information about new babies being born and baptized.
- The crafter creates and maintains the cradle roll banner.

Example #1:
"Babies Online"

A banner with a light blue background is created with little white felt T-shirts hanging on string, with workable mini craft clothespins (which will hold the T-shirt on the banner), to symbolize a clothesline. On each T-shirt, sewn or written in puff paint, include the baby's name, birth date, and Baptism date. On the child's third birthday, the little shirt would be removed and given to the parents as a special keepsake. This will also symbolize the child being ready to enter the preschool Sunday School. Words on the top of the banner would say, "Babies Online @ (name of church)." On the bottom of the banner, in colored, childlike building blocks, it would spell out "BEGINNINGS."

Example #2:
"I Am Jesus' Little Lamb"

A banner with a green background created with white felt sheep silhouettes (with Velcro on the back) and baby's name, birth date, and Baptism date sewn or puff painted on each one. On the child's third birthday, the little lamb would be taken off and given to the parents as a special keepsake. This will also symbolize the child being ready to enter the preschool Sunday School. Words on the banner would say, "I Am Jesus' Little Lamb."

Reflection

Is the banner visually pleasing? Are the names and dates correct? Are the objects on the banner put up and taken down in a timely manner? Is a new banner needed? Is the banner hanging in an appropriate place to be seen often by young families?

Cradle Cooks

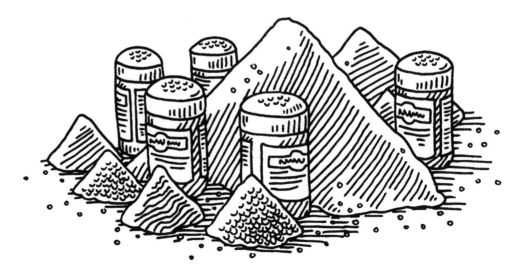

_____
(Church name)

Goal

This group will provide a meal for each family of a newborn at (_name of congregation_).

Purpose

Share the love of Jesus by showing the families that they are loved and cared for by their church and that their newborn is welcomed and celebrated.

Objectives

- Following the guidelines of the cradle cooks job description, a cook would prepare and deliver a delicious and nutritious meal to each family of a newborn in the congregation.
- Members who deliver meals act as ambassadors of the church, building good relationships with each family of a newborn.

Activities

The Director of Children's Ministry will appoint the Cradle Cook Head to organize and oversee the cradle cooks program.

Reflection

Are the meals getting to the families in a timely manner? Is appropriate food being served? Was there compliance for special foods requested? Are there adequate numbers of meal providers? Are acquired cradle cooks geographically located to point of delivery?

REPRODUCIBLE
BLUEPRINT

Cradle Cook Head

Ministry Description

_____
(Church name)

1. Work with the Director of Children's Ministry and the Cradle Coordinator to compile a list of potential cradle cooks. Review cradle cook guidelines.

2. Recruit volunteers willing to make meals for families of newborn babies in the church and instruct them on the procedures and their role as a cradle cook. Consider asking young parents to be cradle cooks so that new relationships can be formed with those similar in age.

3. After receiving information from the Director of Children's Ministry about a new baby being born in the congregation, the Cradle Cook Head will call a cradle cook to provide and deliver a meal to the family.

4. Keep a running record of who cooked for whom and when.

5. Make a follow-up phone call the day after the delivery of the meal to the new mother to congratulate her, make sure she received the meal, and ask if everything was okay with the delivery and the food. If the family would like another meal, contact more cradle cooks.

6. Talk with the cradle cook sometime after the delivery of the meal to thank him or her and make sure everything went well. Encourage the cradle cook to continue building a relationship with the new parents.

7. Determine if one, two, or even three meals will be offered, taking into consideration how many cradle cooks there are and how often babies are born in your congregation. If more than one meal will be delivered, organize a schedule with the cradle cooks so that the meals are spread out over time. An example would be a meal brought Monday, Wednesday, and Friday, or Tuesday and Saturday, depending on the desire of the family and how many meals are being provided.

Cradle Cook

Ministry Description

_____

(Church name)

1. Once a cradle cook receives word from the Cradle Cook Head about a new baby, he or she will call the new parents, offer congratulations, offer a meal to be brought to their home, inquire about likes, dislikes, allergies, and when the family would like the meal brought to their home. Be sure to get directions to the house.

2. Prepare the meal. Follow the information about likes, dislikes, and allergies. Be sure to follow cooking standards of safety using only fresh and well-cooked food. Always wash hands!

3. Deliver the meal to the family in a timely manner. If you say that you will be at their house by 5:00 p.m., be there on time. If something prevents you from following through, let the new mother know as soon as possible.

4. Whenever possible, use disposable dishware to transport the meals so that the new parents have as few dishes to wash as possible. If you do not use throw-away containers, arrange to pick up nondisposable dishware, or ask the parents to bring the dishes to a designated place at church for you to retrieve. You can also arrange a time and place at church to meet in order to get the dishware back so that your relationship can continue and grow.

5. Keep the goal, purpose, and objective in mind when participating in this ministry.

Quiet Room

_____
(Church name)

Goal

Often different from a nursery, this is a place set aside for parents to attend to the needs of their infants or toddlers during a worship service.

Purpose

Knowing that the attention span of young children is short, they are still developing good behaviors and church manners, they are exploring and learning new skills in life, and they have special needs, the church offers this opportunity to help parents during worship. This type of care welcomes babies and children to be a part of worship time in the church.

Objectives

- Parents and children will feel Jesus' love and hear sounds from the worship service.

- Parents will be able to calm their upset child who has become restless in worship.

- Parents will have an opportunity to talk to their young child about worship and refocus their little one before returning to the sanctuary.

- Infants can be rocked, nursed, and have their diapers changed in a private and clean setting.

Activities

A quiet room, close to the sanctuary and readily visible to visiting families, will have the following:

- Appropriate furniture and supplies, including a changing table, diapers, baby wipes, tissues, hand sanitizer, and a small garbage can with a lid. A rocking chair is a great addition to help parents calm their children or for mothers to nurse.

- Sound system installed to hear the worship service.

- One-way window installed for nursing mothers and diaper-changing privacy, yet parents and children have a view of the worship service.

- Inviting yet calming painted walls with a few baby or young childlike wall hangings such as the cradle roll banner, a cross, simple pictures of babies and children, etc.

- Quiet items such as cloth or board books about Jesus, worship, etc.

- Possible signs framed and hanging with words printed that give suggestions of what parents can say to their child about worship as they look out the glass window. Examples include, "Where are the candles? Can you find the cross? See the people giving their gifts to Jesus. Do you hear the choir singing to Jesus? What is the pastor doing? See the people praying to Jesus? Look at the pretty windows. Sometimes we are quiet in church and sometimes we sing."

- Sign on the inside of the room:

  "Welcome to the **quiet room**! This special area is provided for adults who need a place to change their little one's diapers or nurse their babies, or a quiet spot for their child who has become restless during worship. Please remember this room is not soundproof. Loud noises can travel into the sanctuary. You are encouraged to talk to your toddler about worship. This will help your little one to refocus on being a part of family worship. Children are never to be left alone in this room."

"The **nursery** provides child care for parents who prefer to leave their child (three years old and under) in loving, safe, supervised care while they attend worship services, Bible class, or meetings. This room is located *(tell where here)*. Parents receive a pager that will blink if the parent is needed. Please see an usher if you need further assistance."

- Keep the room clean and inviting.
- Provide information to the congregation about this room by newsletter articles, bulletin announcements, and pew cards.

Pew Card Example:

1. *Print the following and cut to size, such as on a 4 × 8-inch heavy paper, laminate, and place one behind the friendship or registration cards in the pews or chairs in the sanctuary. Size so that the words "Parents of Young Children" can be seen right above the cards in front of them. If that is not possible, then decide where best your information should go to be readily and easily seen by parents. Just placing this guide in the bulletin each Sunday will not guarantee the parents seeing this message in a timely manner when they could really use the information early in the worship service.*

Parents of Young Children

(Name of church) welcomes your family to our worship services. We support your desire to teach your small children about worshiping God in His house. We understand that sometimes wiggles can get the best of your little one. During worship, thank you for being sensitive to others around you.

The quiet room is located (state location here). This special area is provided for adults who need a place to change their little one's diapers or nurse their baby, or need a quiet spot for their child who has become restless during worship. You will still be able to hear and see the worship service in this room while comforting your child. This also gives an opportunity to talk encouragingly to your little one about worship.

The nursery is located (state location here) and provides child care for parents who prefer to leave their child (three years old and under) in loving and safe supervised care while attending worship services or Bible class. Parents receive a pager that will vibrate and blink if the parent is needed. Please see an usher for further assistance.

Reflection

Is the room being used? What else would assist the parents of infants and toddlers in that room? Is the room kept clean? Is the sound system working and set at an appropriate volume? How are the ventilation, heating and cooling systems, and lighting? Can parents find the room easily? Is it visitor friendly?

REPRODUCIBLE
BLUEPRINT

Basket of Blessings

(Church name)

Goal

To provide worshipful quiet items for young children while they attend the worship service with their families.

Purpose

Since most young children do not have a long attention span and can become restless in church, they will have items available to help them focus on Jesus during a church service while allowing parents more opportunity for personal worship, especially during the sermon.

Objective

The children will be occupied and engaged while remaining in the church sanctuary to experience worship time with their family and the rest of the congregation.

Activity

A large basket is filled with quiet items to be retrieved by children at the beginning of a worship service and returned when the service ends. Include the following:

- Children's worship bulletins.
- Age-appropriate religious books and children's Bibles with attached stickers that say, "Please return to the Basket of Blessings at (name of church) after the service. Thank you."
- Colored pencils or twistable crayons.
- Pocket folders labeled "Sermon Scribbles" with plain white paper inside.
- Treats for Toddlers: Clear, closing, snack-size plastic bags containing small amounts of dry oat cereal circles or little fish-shaped crackers. Labels on the front would read "Treats for Toddlers" and "Taste and see that the LORD is good! (Psalm 34:8)."

Supplies would be stored in an appropriate place.

Appoint someone to care for this ministry.

Reflection

Are the children using the items in the Basket of Blessings? Is the Basket of Blessings being kept supplied, clean, and orderly? Is the Basket of Blessings placed in an accessible and appropriate place? Are new or more items needed in the basket?

Optional:

> *Create 10 × 12-inch cloth bags with short handle straps for the children to carry their "supplies" into the sanctuary and return after the worship service. Embroider the church name on the front of the worship bags for the little ones to begin recognizing the letters in the name of their church. Purchase or build a stand with knobs for the children to hang their worship bags. The stand can even be made and painted to look like a tree.*

Other options:

Some churches provide a wooden boat that holds church worship bags for the children. Other churches have small wooden coat hangers that hold the bags. Various congregations have a special wooden shelf built to house the worship supplies and children's Bibles that are easily accessible. Still others keep the bags in a basket, set near other children's materials.

Nursery

Goal

To provide a trusting place and trustworthy attendant for young children of members and visitors who need a babysitter at church.

Purpose

Members and visitors will be confident that their young children will be loved and well cared for at church when parents are unable to be with them. This is provided during worship, Bible study, meetings, or any other church event where there is need for child care.

Objectives

- Create an appropriate, comfortable, safe environment for babies and young children.
- Provide qualified, loving nursery attendants and other babysitters when needed.
- Show these little ones, as well as their parents, that the church loves them, cares about them, and church is a place where young children can be happy and excited to come even if they are not in the same room with their parents.

Activities

- Supply the room with needed resources such as safe and clean toys, children's religious books, hand sanitizer, tissues, covered garbage can, small table with child-size chairs, etc.
- Address safety issues, such as covering safety outlets.
- Use inside windows to see into the nursery while in the building.
- Provide pagers that blink for parents to alert them to return to the nursery when needed. Parents sign a pager notebook before taking a pager number.
- Hire carefully screened nursery attendants or babysitters. Complete background checks on all hired nursery attendants and volunteer babysitters. Nursery attendants and babysitters are trained to follow care guidelines.
- Deep cleaning of the room will take place periodically. Simple cleaning and sanitizing will take place after each event.
- A care notebook will be provided for parents to leave information about the care of their child.
- Sound from the sanctuary is streamed into the nursery room so the children and caregiver can hear worship. A CD player with children's religious song CDs can be used for child care outside of worship time.

Reflection

Assessment of the program, facility, and babysitters will be continual.

Optional

It is special to give your nursery a name. For example, stanza three in the hymn "Away in a Manger" says, "Bless all the dear children in Thy tender care" (*LSB* 365). You could call you church nursery the Tender Care Nursery. Have a gifted person in your congregation paint those words from the song on the nursery wall.

Nursery Attendant

Job Description

_____

(Church name)

Goal

The nursery attendant is a warm, loving, friendly, responsible Christian person with knowledge about infant and young child development who is mentally and physically able to protect, care for, and happily play with the little ones who require babysitting at church.

Purpose

The purpose of serving as a nursery attendant at (name of church) is to glorify God by helping to care for the youngest members of the congregation and young visiting children.

Objective

After the church has created a comfortable, safe environment for infants and young children, the nursery attendant will provide proper care for children from birth through age 3 during the worship service, Bible study hour, meetings, and any other events that require a babysitter.

Qualifications

- A Christian who is able to attend worship outside of the Sunday morning child-care time requirement _(Note the youngest age your church is comfortable with filling this position.)_
- Likes children
- Responsible and dependable
- Knowledgeable about infant and child development
- Patient, kind, honest, flexible
- Healthy and physically able to pick up, hold, and care for infants and small children
- Able to think clearly in a crisis
- Communicates well
- Preferably CPR certified
- Has a good, cheerful attitude and disposition so that the children will feel happy, cared for, secure, and comforted
- Desires to develop good relationships with children and their parents

Activities and Specific Responsibilities

1. On the day of service, arrive on time at the designated place. Make sure the room is in order, waste cans are emptied, and any further preparations are completed before the children begin arriving.

2. Welcome the children, and ask the parents or guardians if their child has any special needs.

3. Provide for the children's needs while they are in your care.

4. Make sure a parent or guardian has a page filled out on the Guidelines for My Child Binder, signs in on the Child Check-In Binder, and takes a pager or leaves a cell phone number.

5. Page or text a child's parent or guardian in case of emergency, if the child is inconsolable, when a child needs to use the restroom, needs a diaper change, or some other unresolved issue.

6. Never leave children unattended. Follow the children's ministry safety guidelines.

7. Ensure that all children are safely returned and picked up by their parent or guardian after worship or other event. Be sure all pagers are returned to their dock.

8. Clean and pick up toys, books, crumbs, and spills from the nursery floor and play areas, and dispose of garbage in a covered trash can. Sanitize toys and diaper-changing area.

9. In the work binder, accurately and honestly record time worked. Obtain Director of Children's Ministry's (DCM) signature for worked time approval.

10. If applicable, turn off heat, air conditioning, and lights; close blinds; and lock the door behind you.

11. Obtain the schedule from the DCM. Notify DCM if you are unable to serve on a scheduled day and if supplies or equipment are needed.

12. Monitor that hot beverages, such as coffee, are not brought in the nursery room.

Terms and Conditions

A. The nursery attendant reports to the Director of Children's Ministry.

B. The congregational hiring board (elders or church council) determines wages.

C. Attendant is willing to submit to random drug testing and background check.

D. Child care for Sunday mornings will be from 9:00 a.m. to 12 noon.

E. Attendant can be called at anytime to babysit for events, worship, meetings, or Bible studies.

F. Appropriate, child-friendly attire. Unprofessional or cumbersome clothing is undesired.

G. An attendant will not use a personal cell phone or other personal technical device during work time, but will give children full attention.

H. If sickness or other emergency prevents attendant from working, attendant will contact DCM as soon as possible so that another attendant can be arranged.

I. If attendant is no longer able to keep this position, attendant will notify the DCM in writing at least two weeks prior to resignation and participate in an exit interview.

J. This is not a guaranteed, permanent job. Attendant can be released from this position at any time without reason or previous notice.

Contract

Date:_____

I, _____ (full name), understand and agree to the terms and conditions under the nursery attendant job description of (name of church, city, state). I believe that my qualifications meet the requirements. I am able to fulfill the goal, purpose, objectives, activities, and specific responsibilities listed, and I will do my very best to maintain them.

Signature of new Tender Care Nursery attendant _____

Signature of Director of Children's Ministry _____

Signature of head elder _____

Signature of the pastor _____

Guidelines for My Child

_____
(Church name)

Please print all information legibly. Thank you!

Date _____

My child's name is _____.

My child likes to be called _____.

My child is _____ years old.

Parent name(s): _____

Special instructions I would like the nursery attendant to know and follow:

About crying . . . (If your child cries, please specify how long to wait before paging a parent. Give suggestions on what best comforts your child if he/she does cry.)

_____

_____

_____

About food . . . (Please list any foods you do not want your child to have and any allergies your child has. Give instructions for milk/bottle-fed babies, juice, or any other snack foods your child can eat that are in your diaper bag.)

_____

_____

_____

Please be sure your baby has a clean diaper on before leaving him/her in the nursery, or take your child to the restroom before leaving him/her in the nursery. Parents will be paged if a diaper needs changing or if a child needs to use the restroom, as a nursery attendant will not be able to leave the other children in the nursery.

Please share any concerns or further information that you feel is important for the nursery attendant to know.

Other special instructions:

_____

_____

_____

Parent's signature _____

Child Check-In

Nursery Alert System

_____
(Child ministry)

_____
(Church name)

Please print legibly.

Date	Your Name	Child's Name	Pager or Cell Phone #	Special Instructions

Little Lambs & Ewe

_____

(Church name)

Goal

This is a play group for parents and young children, such as a Mom and Me group.

Purpose

This group will provide Christian caring, sharing, fellowship, and camaraderie for mothers, and playtime and social interaction for their young ones.

Objective

Mothers and their children, from newborn through preschool, gather together twice a month at a designated place and time. Both congregational members and nonmembers are welcome!

Activities

- A coordinator is chosen for organizing and publicizing the gatherings.
- The playgroup meets at parks, playgrounds, zoos, museums, homes, church, etc.
- Dates and times are scheduled.
- Sometimes the group will gather to play and converse, and other times they will choose a special theme or holiday and plan some adventure like teddy bear picnics, spring tricycle races, wagon ride walks, costume parties, Christmas celebration, Valentine's Day cupcake day, a day when grandmothers get to come and play, etc. (The sky is the limit!) Mothers create their own ideas and share with the group as everyone decides what they would like to do or events and places in their area they would like to visit as a group.
- This group relies on each other's donations and/or whatever is allowed in the church budget to help supplement special activities.

Reflection

Is twice a month too often for the group to meet? Is there adequate publicity for this group? Are the mothers forming friendships? If there is a cost for activities, is it being kept to a minimum for everyone? What works well? What could be improved? Are there articles written up in the church newsletters to share about this group and their activities? What other mothers could be invited? Is there an opportunity for a separate group, such as for dads or grandparents?

Children's Christian Education Hour

_____

(Church name)

Goal

Sunday School classes for children, where they will gain knowledge and understanding of God's Word and be able to express their Christian faith in joyful praise, stewardship, and mission activity.

Purpose

Children are nurtured in their faith and grow in their relationship with God and with others.

Objective

Children will become aware of the mighty power and love of God and what He has done for them so that they will desire to continue to follow Him and respond to His love.

Activities

Doctrinally sound curriculum, a Sunday School Head Coordinator, Sunday School Department Coordinator, and qualified teachers are chosen with the assistance of the Director of Children's Ministry and approval of the pastor.

Teachers will teach Bible-centered lessons each Sunday morning to the children including the following:

- Reinforcement of lessons with prepared learning centers and/or creative activities such as art, crafts, drama, videotaping, etc.
- Gathering of offerings
- Presentation and practice of Bible Words to Remember
- Prayer
- Singing of hymns/praise songs

Reflection

Are the children active listeners and participants? What are some things that are working and some things that could use a change? Are the rooms age appropriate and adequate for space and furniture? Do the students know why they are there, what they are doing, and the importance of growing in their knowledge of Holy Scripture? Did every child hear the Gospel message? Are they expressing love for Jesus and thankfulness for His gift of salvation? Are they showing love for one another in words and deeds? Is the teacher being a role model of what has just been taught? Do the Sunday School teachers know the parents and siblings of their students? Are Sunday School teachers developing a good relationship with their students and their families?

Note

Bible Class: A teacher/student learning environment

Bible Study: A less formal setting; leader and participants together work through parts of Scripture

Sunday School Bible Lesson

_____

(Church name)

Goal

Children will gain knowledge and understanding of God's Word.

Purpose

Faith, life application of Scripture, and love for God's Word are developed (Proverbs 22:6).

Objective

Teach children a Bible story or lesson in an age-appropriate manner and give them opportunity to express what they have learned either orally, in action, by behavior, or some creative form.

Activities

- Following the Sunday School Teacher's Guide, tell a Bible account to the class using Scripture with creative forms and visuals age appropriate for the class.

- Help the students apply the Christ-centered Bible teachings to their lives by using oral communication, projects and activities contained in the curriculum provided, and other creative resources.

- Give opportunity for children's participation in conversation, questions, and activities that reinforce the story, objectives, and lesson focus.

Reflection

Is the teacher following and teaching what is true to Scripture? Is proper Law and Gospel being used? Are the students active listeners while the Sunday School teacher is teaching or telling the Bible story? Are the students participating in the projects or activities provided? Do the children demonstrate by their behavior what they have learned, and that they are developing a closer relationship to Jesus as their personal Savior?

Children's Offering

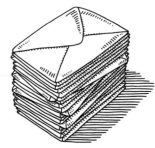

(Church name)

Goal

Children are presented with opportunities to give an offering.

Purpose

A foundation is laid upon which children can build a life of cheerfully sharing their God-given gifts and experience the joy of giving in response to God's love (2 Corinthians 9:7; Matthew 6:21; Matthew 10:42).

Objective

Children are made aware of how their gifts are an act of worship and are used by the church to build God's kingdom.

Activities

- Teach children the practical needs of the church such as electricity, water, Bibles, supplies, pay for staff, the importance of mission activities, and how giving comes from the heart.

- Publicize about monetary offerings or other designated contributions, and gather them at programs such as Sunday School, Vacation Bible School, and Day School chapel.

- Have children take turns gathering the offering and setting it on the altar. A prayer and song may be offered asking God to bless the use of the gifts.

- Supply children with offering envelopes for them to bring their monetary offerings in order that the amount of their gifts would remain between them and God (Matthew 6:1–4). Envelopes also help the children not lose their offerings, especially if they are giving loose change.

- Inform parents about the offerings to help equip them to teach their children how sharing is a wonderful privilege and one way to show love to God.

Reflection

Are the children giving their offerings? Do the children use the envelopes, and are they helpful? Is there good publicity about the offerings? Are the children and their parents aware of how the offerings are being used? Did the offerings or contributions get to their prospective designations in a timely manner? Were any charts or posters used to help show the progress of, motivate, and encourage giving?

When there is an event, like Vacation Bible School or Hearts for Jesus, etc., setting a goal for a certain amount is acceptable. It is also all right to chart or keep track of the giving as a whole group. Wanting to give as an act of worship still occurs. But when giving becomes a competition, such as whether boys or girls can bring the most money, then the godly purpose for giving can become lost. The heart of giving then changes from being a response to God's love to selfishly giving in order to win.

Option

Parents may appreciate the idea of keeping offering envelopes in the car to help them keep stewardship in mind and in an easy-to-remember space.

REPRODUCIBLE
BLUEPRINT

Children's Prayer Time

_____
(Church name)

Goal

As God's dearly loved children, they will talk with Him (Proverbs 15:29; 1 John 5:14).

Purpose

Prayer is commanded by God and is a great privilege for those who believe in Jesus Christ (1 Timothy 2:8).

Objectives

- Teach the children about prayer
- Provide opportunities for the children to pray out loud with others in a group and silently by themselves
- After the teacher instructs the children about prayer, they will be able to pray
    - comfortably out loud.
    - with others in a group.
    - personally by themselves.
    - and know that God hears and answers them for their good.

Activities

- Invite the young children to pray by talking with their heavenly Father (Romans 8:15–16). Pray *mirror prayers* together (the leader says a few words of the prayer at a time and then the children repeat those words).
- As the children grow, teach them more about prayer by helping them learn the following:

1. We pray only to the true God: Father, Son, and Holy Spirit (Exodus 20:3–4).

2. Ways to pray: folded hands/bowed head/closed eyes/crossed or uplifted arms/kneeling (Matthew 6:6).

3. We pray for ourselves and for all other people, even our enemies (Matthew 5:44).

4. God the Holy Spirit prays with and for us (Romans 8:26).

5. There are four types of prayer:

    - *Praise* (Adoration): "Dear God, You are so great!" (Psalm 135:3)
    - *Sorry* (Repentance, confession): "Dear God, I am sorry that I . . ." (Psalm 51:1–2; Ephesians 4:32; Matthew 6:14–15; James 5:16)
    - *Thanksgiving* (Appreciation, grateful heart): "Thank You, God, for . . ." (Psalm 136:1; 1 Thessalonians 5:16–18)
    - *Asking* (Requests for self and others) according to His will: "Dear God, please help . . ." (Psalm 50:15; Matthew 7:7–8; John 16:23; Philippians 4:6; 1 Timothy 2:1–2; 1 John 5:14)

6. Jesus gave us the Lord's Prayer to show us how to pray (Matthew 6:9–15).

7. We pray in Jesus' name (John 16:23).

8. We can pray anywhere, anytime, with anyone and alone, with our family and in church (Matthew 6:6).

9. The Lord invites us to pray often (1 Thessalonians 5:16–18).

10. God always answers our prayers in His own way and in His time (Isaiah 65:24).

11. We end our prayers with *amen*, which means, "Yes! It will be so!" It says that God, in whom we have faith and trust and who has told us to pray, will hear our prayers and answer them as He has promised.

- Offer opportunities to pray with others and out loud at the beginning, middle, and end of Sunday School class and other events and any time and place the children are together.

- Have the children share about times they have prayed to God or about other times they could pray to Him.

- Ask the children why they think talking with God is important and what it means.

- Practice special ways to pray such as *circle prayers* (stand in a circle holding hands and taking turns around the circle saying each one's own prayer out loud); *popcorn prayers* (children stay where they are and each person says a prayer in no particular order); writing prayers out on a big sheet of paper for others to also pray; and so on. Encourage silent prayers for times in the car, at bedtime, in school, on vacation, on the playground, and the like.

Reflection

Do the children volunteer to pray out loud? Are they anxious to talk with their heavenly Father? How often does prayer time take place at the various events including Sunday School? Is prayer time happening before and after practices, before a special presentation like the family Christmas worship service, singing in church, etc.? Are thank-You prayers being offered often? Do all children have the opportunity to share their requests for certain prayers?

Optional: Begin a K.I.P. (Kids in Prayer) Club. Elementary children gather to learn more about prayer and talk with God together.

Other activities may include these:

- Provide kids with paper and writing instruments to write prayers and put them in their own prayer box that they made.

- Have a bulletin board where kids can post prayers for others to pray with them.

- Gather a small group of kids to stand in a circle, shoulder to shoulder. Have them lean forward extending their arms out in the middle so the palms of their hands are up and their fingertips are touching the other children's. Place the P, R, A, and Y letters of some building blocks in the middle of all their hands. Stand on a sturdy chair or ladder in order to take a top view of their arms and hands holding the word pray. Post it on your prayer bulletin board.

- Have the kids pray for someone in the congregation. Then, have them make cards for that person including words that say they are praying for them.

- Tape a large sheet of butcher paper on a wall or door for kids to write all the things they are thankful for as one big thank-You prayer to God. Make sure your paper is thick enough if they use markers. You do not want the writing to bleed through the paper and onto the wall or door.

- Create an action between those participating. Have the kids gently bump each other's fists as they say "KIP!" as a reminder to keep talking with God.

Children's Music

(Church name)

Goal

The children express their Christian faith in joyful praise and song.

Purpose

Children give glory to God through sound, enjoy participating in God's gift of music, and enrich others with their praise in worship services and other gatherings (Colossians 3:16).

Objective

Teach the children various songs and instrumental pieces and lead them in joyfully praising God together.

Activities

- The Sunday School provides Christian music opportunities for the children such as learning hymns, songs of praise, handbells, rhythm sticks, praising scarves, and other forms of musical expression, and schedules occasions to share that in worship services.

- The music leader of Vacation Bible School or other ministry opportunities teaches the children thematic songs and other appropriate music and offers opportunities to share that music with others, especially at the closing program.

- Kids' Night Out—Bible Blast! provides a music, singing, and praise time opportunity.

- Children's choirs are established and then given the opportunity to enhance worship services with their praise.

Reflection

Are the children enjoying their music experiences and praise opportunities? Are the songs and activities age appropriate and uplifting? Are the songs and hymns faithful and Christ-centered? Is there good child attendance for singing in worship? Is the music budget adequate? Do choir/music directors/leaders fulfill their responsibilities? Do Sunday School teachers use music to reinforce their lessons, or do they need more resources? Are the facilities adequate for music environment? How is the children's choir developing?

Optional: Name your various age-grouped choirs (Church Mouse Choir, Little Lights Choir, Kids' Praise Choir, Sonshine Singers, Joyful Youth, etc.).

Children's Choir Director

Ministry Description

_____
(Church name)

1. The children's choir director will be a member of the church who is committed to faithful worship, Bible study, and prayer.

2. The director will do the following.

   - Have an understanding of the Children's Music Blueprint.

   - Use a smile and joyful heart to let the love of Jesus radiate through the songs you present, teach, and lead.

   - Determine where and when the children's choir will meet. Make the necessary arrangements. Teach age-appropriate songs and sing with the children for an age-appropriate amount of time. Plan water fountain or restroom breaks if needed.

   - Explain the words to the songs so that the children know what they are singing.

   - Use piano, guitar, organ, CDs, instruments, or whatever or whoever is available or needed for musical accompaniment. Children may be invited to play instruments that they are gifted in or have ability to accompany the children's choir.

   - Work with the DCM for resources needed and reflection on how the choir is progressing.

   - Prior to teaching a song to be sung in a worship service, make arrangements for the date and service when you would like the children to sing, and provide the words for pastoral approval. Present the words of the approved song to whoever prepares the church bulletin for inclusion in the service folder.

   - Strive to sing in a minimum of four worship services a year.

   - Keep the parents informed of the choir schedule and when the children will be singing in church.

   - Maintain a record of practice times, attendance, when the children sing for worship or other events, and what songs they sang.

   - Know the children's choir budget and use funds wisely. Work with the DCM during budget planning time to plan for next year's children's choir budget proposal.

   - Recruit teen or adult helpers when needed.

   - Continue to invite other children to join the children's choir.

Bible Words to Remember

_____

(Church name)

Goal

The children are equipped with words of Scripture to keep in their minds and hearts that they will be able to draw on throughout their lives and in all their circumstances.

Purpose

Throughout their lives, children will be able to do the following.

- Safeguard God's Word in their hearts (Psalm 119:11)
- Hold onto the Word as treasure in their lives (Colossians 2:2–3)
- Use God's Word as a guide for their lives (Psalm 119:105)
- Experience God's comfort in times of trouble or trial (John 14:1; 1 Peter 4:12–13)
- Teach and admonish others with wisdom (Colossians 3:16)
- Share God's Word with others by recalling it from memory (1 Peter 3:15)

Objective

The children will learn a specific Bible passage (and parts of the catechism if applicable) and then be motivated and encouraged to recite it from memory.

Activities

- Determine age-appropriate Bible Words to Remember and assign weekly—utilizing the curriculum.
- Mail or send home with the children a special note to the parents, sharing with them the assigned Bible passages and the goal, objective, and purpose of being able to recall Scripture.
- Sunday School teachers or special adult helpers listen to memory work being recited each Sunday in Sunday School. Vacation Bible School teachers can do this daily throughout the week. Other children's event leaders in the church can adopt the same idea to fit their program.
- Teach about the honor we show for God's Holy Word, the Bible. Open a Bible up and show the children God's very Word. Talk in a soft, slow voice to emphasize sacredness and importance. Have the children actually touch His written Words in an honoring and respectful way.
- Be wary of tangible rewards or prizes. These things can set up unhealthy competition and become an enticement that may overshadow the goal. Strive to keep "holding God's Word in their heart as treasure" as the motivation. Create a big red poster board heart where children can all place a Bible sticker on each week after saying their Bible Words. It is a great way to show how much Scripture they keep hiding in their hearts as time progresses. Very young nonreaders may take a while to warm up to "repeating out loud." Even if they can only say one little word out of the passage, praise them and let them add a sticker. Stay positive and encouraging. A foundation is being put down for desiring God's Word to be in their minds and hearts.
- Review meaning and application for our lives, explain any new or big words in next week's "Bible Words to Remember" and how it relates to our lives, and help the children to understand the meaning of the passage.
- When applicable, add motions to the Scripture passages to help the children remember the words. Drawing and painting a picture can also enrich the memory experience.

Reflection

Are the children learning their memory work? Are the children showing signs of application or recalling their verses that relate to new lessons being taught? Is there parental support? Does more information need to be given to parents? Do the children understand why they are memorizing and the importance and blessing of this privilege?

Sunday School Head Coordinator

Ministry Description

_____
(Church name)

1. A member of the church who is committed to faithful worship, Bible study, and prayer.

2. This person is responsible, along with the Director of Children's Ministry (DCM), for special worship services and events that involve the Sunday School. His or her tasks include the following:

- Create and work with the DCM on a spending plan for the yearly budget. Keep an ongoing record of the expenses.

- Work with the DCM and the pastor to select Sunday School teachers, substitutes, assistants, and ministry coordinators, and then recruit, support, encourage, and pray for them. Communicate and consult with the DCM when questions arise or there is a need for guidance with specific issues or ideas needed in the Sunday School classroom.

- Create a list of and train substitute teachers. Make this list available for Sunday School teachers. Provide phone numbers of substitute teachers for the Sunday School teachers to call if they need a substitute to teach for them. Have teachers inform you when this happens and who will teach.

- Be available during the Sunday School hour as a resource for disciplinary matters, shortages of supplies, bathroom needs, and any other classroom concerns. Help guests and new students to find their classroom, and introduce them to the teacher.

- Hold Sunday School teachers accountable to their job description. Help the Department Coordinator when needed (vacancy or illness, etc.).

- Delegate volunteers to assist with administrative responsibilities and other areas when needed.

- Hold monthly Sunday School teacher meetings. Provide resources and training for the teachers and substitutes.

- Order, obtain, and distribute curricular materials and other needed resources.

- Observe teachers and evaluate classroom facilities.

- Seek the assistance of the DCM to create, provide, and update Sunday School registration forms and release of liability, indemnity agreement, and consent for medical treatment forms for students in the Sunday School. Know where they are stored in case of emergency.

- When purchasing resources, use the church's federal ID number for tax exemption.

- Meet with the DCM and Sunday School teachers to decide the designation of the offerings, be responsible for communication to the students and their parents about the offering designation, and send the offerings to the recipients in a timely manner.

- Direct or recruit directors, along with the DCM and obtained pastoral approval, for the family Christmas worship service and any other special worship and events (such as rally day or Christian education Sunday) that require a director or coordinator in the Sunday School.

- Keep in constant communication with the DCM.

- Communicate news of the Sunday School to the congregation through the Sunday bulletins, church newsletter, and church website. (Be careful when publicly displaying pictures. Only post pictures of those individuals who have given their written permission. Children's pictures need written parental permission to be put on view. Large group pictures where individuals are unrecognizable are acceptable to show.)

- With the help of the DCM, attend and promote outside Sunday School workshops, conferences, and other enrichment events for the Sunday School teachers.

- Quarterly, provide the DCM with attendance records and offering amounts.

- Find ways to encourage the Sunday School staff and keep them and the children of the Sunday School uplifted in prayer.

REPRODUCIBLE BLUEPRINT

Sunday School Department Coordinator

Ministry Description

(Church name)

1. The Sunday School Department Coordinator is a member of the church who is committed to faithful worship, Bible study, and prayer.

2. The tasks for this ministry include the following:

   - Assist the Sunday School classroom teachers by providing resources such as Bibles and art supplies that are needed each Sunday for the Sunday School.

   - Identify storage areas and safely store needed Sunday School resource materials used by all of the individual classes.

   - Create and keep a continual and updated master roster of the children in the Sunday School. This should include their birthday, baptismal birthday, parents' names, address, and telephone numbers. (This information can be obtained from the children's ministry directory.) Distribute to the pastor, the Director of Children's Ministry (DCM), the Sunday School Head Coordinator, and all Sunday School teachers.

   - Participate in and be ready to help with special worship and event activities such as a Christian education Sunday or rally day, the Fall Harvest Fellowship, a family Christmas worship service, or the New Life Festival when needed.

   - Two months before the end of each quarter, notify the Sunday School Head Coordinator of the amount of curricula needed for the next quarter for each class.

   - Create, maintain, distribute, and collect attendance folders every Sunday from each Sunday School class. Keep good attendance records. If needed, help Sunday School teachers mail out "We miss you" cards and missed lesson materials to absent students. Give attendance reports to the Sunday School Head Coordinator.

   - Help the Sunday School Head Coordinator inform the children of where the designated weekly Sunday School offerings will be going. Give the Sunday School Head Coordinator the number of children's offering envelope boxes to order and then distribute the envelope boxes to the children when the boxes arrive. Collect the offerings from the classrooms, record the total amount given, and place the offerings in the church safe or other designated area. Give new students their envelope box and explain about the offerings. Make an ongoing evaluation of the children's offering program.

   - Help assist substitute teachers with resources needed.

   - Attend Sunday School teacher meetings when necessary, assist the Sunday School Head Coordinator, and work with the special ministry coordinators when needed.

   - Keep the Sunday School staff and children uplifted in prayer.

(Church name)
Sunday School Registration

Please PRINT and return to your child's Sunday School teacher. Thank you!

Today's date _____

Parents' names _____

Address _____

Home phone _____

Cell phone (*List whose phone this # belongs to.*) _____

Email _____

Child's full name _____

Date of birth _____

Baptismal date _____

Current age _____

Current grade _____

Special information and/or needs (food allergies, physical limitations, etc.):

_____

_____

_____

Photo release:

(*Church name*) occasionally has the opportunity to use photos to promote the Sunday School and other church activities. Use might include bulletin board, church newsletter, church scrapbook, etc. Please sign to give (*church name*) permission to include your child in photos used for informational or promotional purposes.

Parent signature _____

Sunday School Teacher

Ministry Description

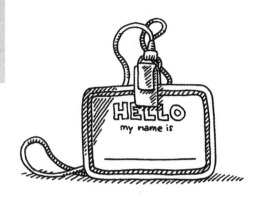

_____
(Church name)

1. This is a member of the church who is committed to faithful worship, Bible study, and prayer.

2. Tasks include the following:

   - Provide a safe, loving, and nurturing learning environment in the classroom that promotes faith development. Follow Safety Guidelines, Discipline, and Personal Peacemaking Blueprints.

   - Prepare and present the Sunday School lessons, utilizing the teacher's guide as provided and any other creative means available. If you have questions about the lesson you will teach, seek help from the Sunday School Head Coordinator, the DCM, or the pastor. Know the lesson well and be ready to share God's very Word with the children. Make sure all children hear the Gospel in every lesson and know that Jesus loves them.

   - Work with the Sunday School Department Coordinator to gather appropriate materials needed for the lesson before class time begins. (Bibles, pencils, flannelgraph, puppets, CD player, markers, scissors, glue, tape, construction paper, stickers, and so on).

   - Be in the classroom plenty of time before class begins in order to develop relationships with the children and to provide supervision and transition into the Sunday School lesson.

   - Record attendance and collect offerings and give them to the department coordinator. Recognize each student's birthday and Baptism birthday in a timely manner.

   - Bring the students to the choir area for opening time or singing. Be on hand to assist the person leading the music. Contact the music coordinator if any extra music or song resources are available for classroom use.

   - Motivate, encourage, and guide the children with their Bible Words to Remember.

   - Maintain classroom control.

   - Keep in good communication with the Sunday School Head Coordinator and notify him/her when there will be a substitute teacher, when questions arise, and if there is a need for guidance with specific issues in the classroom.

   - Help plan and participate in special Sunday School worship and event opportunities and fellowship activities in the Sunday School.

   - Mail Sunday School lessons and "We missed you!" notes to children who were absent. The Department Coordinator can assist when needed. Give a phone call to parents if their child is absent more than two Sundays in a row to show you care and that you are sincerely interested in the spiritual development of the child.

   - Continually assess the progress of the children in your Sunday School class. Stay in communication with parents on how their child is progressing. Return the classroom space to good condition as it was found before the children entered the room.

   - Assimilate new students into the class and make them feel welcomed.

   - Attend Sunday School teacher meetings.

   - Keep the Sunday School, your students, and their parents in prayer.

   - Smile A LOT!

Children's In-Reach/ Outreach Coordinator

Ministry Description

(Church name)

1. This coordinator is a member of the church who is committed to faithful worship, Bible study, and prayer.

2. He or she is friendly, outgoing, and personable with knowledge of the children's ministry program and the Sunday School system.

3. He or she is visible after worship services and aware of visiting children.

4. Tasks include the following:

   - Meet, greet, and invite all visitor children to Sunday School or another children's ministry program or event. Find out if they have visited before or if this is their first time.

   - Create, with the assistance of the Director of Children's Ministry, and offer all first-time visitors a welcome packet. This folder or packet would contain items such as a special pencil or sticker, information about children's ministry and upcoming events or programs, maps, Sunday School or VBS registration forms, and the like. Retrieve completed Sunday School registration forms and give to the Sunday School Department Coordinator.

   - Direct and, if possible, escort parents and their child to where their child's new Sunday School class meets (or where the children's ministry event is taking place). Introduce them to the teacher or leader, and indicate where the child can be picked up again.

   - Provide Sunday School teachers with extra welcome packets for visitors who might have gotten missed. Provide Sunday School teachers or other leaders with "We're so glad you came!" notes or postcards for teachers to follow up with students. Encourage teachers to follow up with their visitors.

   - Review the list of children in the children's ministry directory who are eligible for Sunday School. Periodically mail out invitation cards and call and invite those not actively attending Sunday School. Come alongside the parents of those children for encouragement in attending Sunday School and Sunday morning adult Bible class for themselves.

   - Be involved with promoting children's ministry, Sunday School, VBS, and any other related children's program or event in and outside the church. Include invitations and announcements to the church preschool or elementary school.

   - Obtain and keep a mailing list of all visiting children from special events such as Vacation Bible School, New Life Festival, Kids' Night Out—Bible Blast!, and the like. Follow up with "Glad you came!" notes and send them invitations for Sunday School and other future events and activities.

   - Attend children's ministry meetings and Sunday School teacher meetings when needed.

   - Work with special ministry coordinators and attend meetings when needed.

Christian Education Sunday

Sunday School Rally Day/Jump Day

_____

(Church name)

Goal

A day is set aside for members to gather together at church to celebrate and mark the beginning of a new year in the area of Christian education.

Purpose

After a day of celebration giving thanks to God for His Word:

- The children of the Sunday School will be excited to begin the new Sunday School year.
- Parents will be motivated to bring their children to Sunday School and to attend adult Bible class themselves.
- The congregation will be inspired to join faith-nurturing opportunities and support the Sunday School, Day School, and preschool.

Objective

The congregation will unite and encourage Sunday School and Bible study attendance and gain gratitude and renewed enthusiasm for all its Christian education opportunities.

Activities

The Director of Children's Ministry and the Sunday School Head Coordinator will work together with the pastor (and the school principal, if applicable) in planning how this day will be carried out.

- Choose and display the theme of the year.
- Register new Sunday School children, and update those children already attending Sunday School.
- Encourage faithful Sunday School attendance; inform about curriculum, confirmation class, and teen and adult Bible studies.
- Plan what will take place during worship, how the children and choirs will participate.
- Plan what will happen during the Bible study hour: when children "jump" to the next class level or receive Bibles or catechisms; when leaders acknowledge all children for attendance, introduce teachers, and announce new classrooms. Possibly have a long jump rope with two people turning the rope for the children to really "jump" to their next level. As the rope is turned, those leaving the eighth grade and "jumping" to the senior youth level may "run" through the jump rope into the arms of the youth group waiting on the other side to embrace the new youth to show that they are welcomed and accepted into the youth group with joy.
- Work with the church Fellowship Board to plan the celebration picnic meal.
- Pastor installs child ministry volunteers (Sunday School teachers, helpers, coordinators, and so on) and youth and adult Bible study leaders. Decide when preschool and day school teachers, directors, and the principal will be installed and how all will participate in events associated with Christian education Sunday to unite church and school.

Reflection

How was the day received? What worked well? Are there any changes or additions to recommend for next year? Is it beneficial to keep rally day and Christian education Sunday the same day, or should they be two separate Sundays?

Children's Fall Harvest Fellowship

_____
(Church name)

Goal

A Children's Fall Harvest Fellowship event is provided in autumn.

Purpose

The children build new Christian relationships and further the bond in those relationships already begun.

Objective

The children interact with each other celebrating God's blessings of the fall season.

Activities

- Determine who will be the leader or coordinator for this activity.
- Plan and provide games, crafts, pumpkin carving, bobbing for apples, farm animals, hayride, singing, food, and other activities for participation.
- Reserve a park or playground for the event to be held. Directional maps for families are distributed.
- Determine the cost; check on budget for available funds and schedule date and time.
- Encourage people to invite their friends and neighbors.
- Arrange cleanup duty.
- Publicize the event.

Reflection

Was there good participation? What worked well this year that we would want to do again? What are some things we will want to change or do new next year? Did the children have fun with each other?

Optional:

- Plan activities for whole family participation.
- Reformation-themed activities can be included.

The Family Christmas Worship Service

_____

(Church name)

Goal

Children of the congregation participate in and present an uplifting, visual, age-appropriate worship service celebrating Jesus' birth.

Purpose

Children of the congregation witness their faith by singing, speaking, and acting in front of the congregation; the congregation is edified.

Objectives

- The children in preschool through sixth-grade Sunday School and other interested children lead the family Christmas worship service. (The two-year-old class could be represented with a video or pictures on screen. Provide special pews for two-year-olds and their families to observe so they can see what they will get to participate in next Christmas when they become "big kids.")

- Sunday School teachers, other child ministry volunteers, youth, and other adults are involved where possible and appropriate.

Activities

- The Sunday School Head Coordinator and the DCM either lead or appoint a director.

- Work with the DCM to select a Christmas worship service.

- Director follows the job description blueprints, schedules practices, and keeps the pastor, DCM, Sunday School Head Coordinator, and parents informed.

Reflection

Was the worship service well received by the congregation? How well did the children participate? What are some things that worked well? What improvements can be made for next year? Were there adequate practice times? Was there enough money in the budget to cover the cost of props and costumes?

Special note:

The family Christmas worship service is geared toward involving children, teens, and adults (the family of God) whose participation enhances the worship service of the congregation.

A children's Christmas service is worship time with special participation of the children and their presentation of the Christmas story (or something related to that theme) and singing.

A children's Christmas program is something that the children present for the purpose of entertainment with no or very little participation of those assembled.

A Christmas pageant is an elaborate and spectacular production.

The Family Christmas Worship Service Director

Ministry Description

_____
(Church name)

1. The director will be a member of the church who is committed to faithful worship, Bible study, and prayer.

2. Work with the DCM to select a Christmas service.

3. Seek pastoral approval of the worship service, and schedule the date and time for the service.

4. Estimate the cost involved in producing this service, and find out what funds are available in the budget for this service.

5. Initiate thoughts to the Sunday School Head Coordinator about small children's gifts at the conclusion of the service to be given out by Sunday School teachers. (Remember that the youth and teachers like them too!) This is something to keep in mind when deciding on budget.

6. Present the ideas to and work with the Sunday School teachers and children's choir directors.

7. Schedule practices. Choose dates and times, reserve facilities, and conduct those practices.

8. Arrange for special props and supplies, such as sewing costumes and borrowing a spotlight or anything else that will be needed.

9. Be in contact with the organist or any other instrumentalists who are needed, and present music for them to practice (including the person responsible for the sound system).

10. Keep the DCM and the Sunday School Head Coordinator updated on the progress of the service planning and practices.

11. Inquire who will type and print out the service as a bulletin or service folder. By what date does that person need the information? In a timely manner, give that person the final outline of the service to publish.

12. If the service is to be recorded, recruit and instruct that person for filming. Flash pictures can be distracting.

13. Be responsible for any informational flyers.

14. Follow up after the service to make sure props and costumes are returned to proper storage.

15. Keep a copy of the bulletin and any other additional information in a folder for future years. Give to the DCM for filing.

The Children's Christmas Jesus' Birthday Party

_____
(Church name)

Goal

This is a birthday party at church carried out in Jesus' honor.

Purpose

To offer opportunity for Christian fellowship and participation in a festive celebration centered on Jesus' birth.

Objectives

- Sunday School Head Coordinator, Sunday School teachers, and DCM work together to plan, organize, set up, and prepare for the event.

- Involve fourth-, fifth-, and sixth-grade Sunday School children in the preparation where possible and appropriate.

Activities

Celebrations may vary from year to year.

- The designated area is decorated and prepared for celebration.

- Food tables can include fruit plate, vegetable platter, chips, meats, dips, and cake with punch or chocolate milk.

- After the family Christmas worship service, all those in attendance are invited for the celebration.

- The Sunday School teachers may present their students with a small Christmas gift.

- The children may assemble around the birthday cake and sing "Happy Birthday" to Jesus.

Reflection

Was there good participation? What worked well this year that we would want to do again? What are some things that should be changed for next year? Were there enough tables set up? Were there adequate decorations, paper supplies, and such? Did we run out of food or was much food left over? Was there music playing in the background?

Optional:

This celebration can be done on a Saturday as an outreach event, including the telling of the Christmas account in Luke 2 and other special games and activities.

Hearts for Jesus

_____

(Church name)

Goal

Throughout the month of February, the children will express their Christian faith through mission activities.

Purpose

An opportunity for children to respond to the command of Jesus as recorded in Matthew 28:19; a chance to help others in need, to learn the meaning of Proverbs 19:17, and to help people in other parts of the world with some of their physical needs and especially their spiritual need to hear about the Savior of all, Jesus Christ.

Objective

After learning about a foreign or a national mission project, the children will share their love for Jesus with people throughout the world through prayer and contributions.

Activities

- Appoint someone to publicize and coordinate this project.

- This mission project will be chosen for February participation. (Project ideas are available through many church body organizations.) The coordinator will work with the DCM for direction.

- Make plans and obtain project materials for prayers and contribution ideas (Valentine's Day bake or craft sales, collection boxes, and the like).

- Information and materials are shared with the Sunday School teachers and children, then posted and publicized for the congregation for added support and contributions.

- After the response of giving is complete, contributions will be sent. Write a letter stating the amount contributed and showing appreciation for the opportunity to respond to this mission project need. Send the letter with the contribution.

- The children and the congregation are informed about the conclusion of the project and the impact it made.

Reflection

Was information given in an informative, creative, and timely manner where the children and the congregation understood what the mission project was and how they could contribute? What kind of participation was there? Did the mission project recipients provide enough information and materials for this project?

Optional:

Pictures are taken of the activity of the children in this project and presented on a bulletin board or placed in an album for inspiration and future reference.

Children's Lenten Art Show

_____
(Church name)

Goal

During the Church season of Lent, religious artwork, created by the children of the congregation, is displayed for others to see.

Purpose

The children will be able to use their God-given creative abilities to witness and share the account of Jesus.

Objective

The children will complete a picture or some other art form of one of the Bible stories from the Passion of Christ.

Activities

- Someone is appointed to publicize, coordinate, and arrange for the display and return of the artwork.

- Children in preschool through sixth grade will be invited to participate in an art show. Letters will be sent home with the Sunday School children, and announcements will be placed in the newsletter and worship service folders about the guidelines for entries.

- Frame the pictures and display the sculptures in an appropriate area for viewing.

- Guidelines and directions are given to the parents of children in the congregation.

- Also give the preschool and day school children an opportunity to contribute.

Reflection

Was there good participation? Were the guidelines simple and understandable? Were the pictures or sculptures well displayed in an appropriate and protected area?

Optional:

To thank and encourage the children, each entry will be given a ribbon for recognition of participation at a set time and date.

Optional:

Hold a few art classes to teach the children about color, line, sky meets ground, vanishing point, and how to hold and paint with a brush, and then give them all a framed canvas to create a painting themed around their favorite Bible story. Call it "Paint and Praise" or "Canvas and Cookies." Soft religious music could be played in the background and a special treat like a cookie could end the sessions.

Special note:

The difference between a craft and art:

- Art requires more creative thought than a craft.

- Craft requires more technical skill than art.

- But the more skill, the better the art.

- And the more creative thought, the better the craft.

- Art is original and a craft is usually a duplicate.

Children's Lenten Art Show

Participation Information

_____
(Church name)

_____
(City and state)

A special Sunday School children's art show will be held here at (name of church) throughout the Lenten season. The theme will be "Our Lord's Passion." All children in preschool through sixth grade are eligible to participate.

Suggested titles include:

- Jesus Riding through Jerusalem on Palm Sunday
- Jesus Washing the Disciples' Feet
- The Last Supper
- Jesus Praying in the Garden of Gethsemane
- The Arrest of Jesus
- Betrayal of Judas (thirty pieces of silver, Judas's kiss of betrayal)
- Peter Cutting Off the High Priest's Slave's (Malchus) Right Ear
- Jesus Before Pontius Pilate
- The Crowd Choosing Barabbas
- Peter's Denial of Jesus
- The Whipping and Mocking of Jesus
- The Crucifixion Procession
- Jesus on the Cross
- Jesus' Burial in the Tomb
- Jesus Rose from the Dead

- *Acceptable forms of media are pencil, pen, charcoal, crayons, markers, Cray-Pas, chalk, tempera or acrylic paints, watercolors, or any combination of these. Pictures should be drawn on 10 × 12-inch poster board or 8½ × 11-inch white heavy paper. Pictures will be matted after being received and will then be displayed. Entries must be at the church no later than Sunday, (date).*

If you have any questions, please contact your child's Sunday School teacher or (DCM's name) at (phone number). It is our hope that all the children of (name of church) will participate in this special event.

OUR LORD'S PASSION

Title: _____

Name: _____

Grade: _____

New Life Festival

(Church name)

Goal

The day before Easter, the Good News of the resurrection of our Lord Jesus is shared with and impressed upon fellow members, guests, and visitors in the community in a Christian Easter activity-based event.

Purpose

- The New Life Festival is a mission opportunity for the people of the congregation to bring unchurched friends to hear the Gospel and to invite them to continue the celebration of victory the next day in Easter Sunday worship.

- The New Life Festival enables the church to carry out its mission statement and vision.

- Volunteers get to use "tools" and visual objects in many creative ways in order to teach about the Church seasons of Lent and Easter.

- Here is where the children become involved with and learn about the Church seasons of Lent and Easter through multisensory learning experiences that leave a lasting impression. The concept of the resurrection becomes very real and meaningful.

- Many of the Sunday School children and members of the church may be familiar with things being taught at the New Life Festival. Now they are given a chance to experience it, live it, and share it with others!

- It is a great occasion to promote Vacation Bible School for the upcoming summer.

- The children, teens, and adults of the church are given an opportunity to start a relationship with others and witness to those hearing and learning about Jesus for the first time.

- The Sunday School teachers, child ministry volunteers, and other volunteers have an opportunity for acts of love and to interact and build relationships with other children outside the church.

- This is a great opportunity to encourage participation in Sunday School, adult Bible study, Sunday worship, and Day School or preschool.

- It is a wonderful Christian fellowship activity outside the Sunday morning schedule.

Objectives

- Through multisensory learning activities and worship time, those attending will gain understanding of the many traditions and symbols of Easter.

- The resurrection of our Lord is celebrated with fellow members, while at the same time the Gospel is shared with visitors.

Activities

- Opening worship in sanctuary for all.

- Babysitting available for those younger than two years of age. Special celebration center for one-year-olds and a parent. One parent also stays with their two-year-old at center rotations.

- Celebration centers (ten minutes each) for children age 2 through sixth grade (coloring eggs, egg roll game, cross experience, food, plants, animals, butterfly craft, Easter egg hunt, and so on). Centers are led by adult child ministry volunteers.

- Teen volunteers help guide the children to and during their centers.

- Youth and adult Bible study or other adult faith-enriching experience such as an art experience, Christian video, or Easter banner making.

- Closing worship and outdoor balloon release for all.

Reflection

How well is the program attended? Are people bringing friends? Are new activities needed in the centers? How smoothly did everything run? Was there enough publicity? Is there enough funding?

Child Ministry Volunteer Training & Support

(Church name)

Goal

Child ministry volunteers gain training.

Purpose

- To communicate
- To be inspired, equipped, empowered, and encouraged to serve children and help children do ministry
- To build relationships with other volunteers and become TEAM players as the Body of Christ (1 Corinthians 12:12–31)

Objective

After training sessions, workshops, and meetings, child ministry volunteers will be prepared to nourish children in the faith and help equip children for living out their Christian lives.

Activities

- Sunday School teacher meetings
- Sunday School workshops
- Meetings and training before special programs (e.g., the family Christmas worship service)
- Meetings and training before events (e.g., Vacation Bible School)
- Children's ministry meetings
- Children's ministry workshops
- Training for new volunteers to be instructed in policies, guidelines, procedures, and the blueprints of their specific area in ministry

Reflection

Are informational sheets available? Do volunteers attend regularly? What will inspire the volunteers to attend? Do the volunteers understand the training and are they able to carry out the activities? How will new volunteers be trained? Do the teacher or leader guides need to be discussed? Are visuals used and examples given in the meetings and workshops? What current topics would be most beneficial for child ministry volunteers? Does the meeting time best serve the participants, or should the meeting times and dates be moved? Do the workshops or in-service gatherings require a meal or refreshments?

Please note:

A *meeting* is typically an hour to an hour and a half long gathering to inform and discuss a specific topic.

Training prepares, teaches, guides, and instructs for a specific activity or event.

Workshops or *in-service* gatherings are extended enrichment opportunities.

Kids' Night Out— Bible Blast!

_____

(Church name)

Goal

This event is a Bible-based fun night for children in preschool through the sixth grade.

Purpose

For faith growth, friendship, and happy times for member children and an outreach to other children guests

Objective

While eating, playing, and learning from a Bible DVD curriculum or other means of Bible learning, the children will grow in their relationship with God and gain knowledge and understanding of God's Word. They will also experience Christian fellowship, opportunities for witnessing their faith, joyful praise time, and putting their love for God into action. They will enjoy the company and personal interaction of child ministry volunteers and other children on the church campus in a safe and familiar environment.

Activities

- Five Wednesday nights per school year. Prepare publicity, registration, and nametags.
- Cost is $3.00 per child per night. (This covers the cost of the curriculum, pizza, and beverages.)
- Decorations depict the theme.
- All gather together for pizza and beverages. (Remember the hand sanitizer.) Games follow. Divide into groups for the Bible lesson. Allow 15 minutes for eating, 15 minutes for playing games, and 45 minutes for Bible lesson, singing, and use of curriculum.
- Near the end, it's time to circle up (review, sing, and pray)!
- Dismiss the children to their parents and send home any crafts created that night.
- Clean up.

Reflection

Do the children and parents benefit from this event? What is the enrollment like? Are there enough volunteers? Do we have enough games to play? Do the children enjoy themselves? Are the children attentive and do they participate? Are we pleased with the curriculum? Are children coming who do not have a home church? Are children from the preschool/day school attending? Is this event centered on the Bible and focused on Christ?

Vacation Bible School (VBS)

_____

(Church name)

Goal

This Gospel- and grace-geared Bible experience is held in the summer, or other vacation time, for children of the congregation and children of the community.

Purpose

To fulfill Jesus' command to make disciples of all nations (Matthew 28:19), which includes children

Objectives

Intentional relationship building with Jesus and others through opportunities for children to do the following:

- Grow in their knowledge and understanding of God's Word.

- See their need for a rescuer from sin, and build a heart-to-heart relationship with their Savior, Jesus Christ.

- Celebrate the joy of praising God.

- Express their faith through a mission project.

- Invite unchurched friends to hear and learn about God.

- Fellowship together.

Activities

- The Director of Children's Ministry will either direct VBS or appoint a VBS director and a planning committee who will evaluate various VBS curricula and choose one with pastoral approval.

- The VBS director and planning committee will consult with the Director of Children's Ministry for deciding on VBS dates, creating registration forms, publicity, recruiting volunteers, guidance, creating props, ordering supplies and resources, choosing and publicizing about a

mission project, overseeing the VBS program as a whole, holding any necessary VBS meetings, and planning a schedule for the VBS program, which will include the following:

- Opening; worship; music praise time; skits; mission project

- Age-appropriate Bible lesson with visuals

- Craft or science-based learning activity to reinforce the Bible lesson

- Treats with friendship-building time

- Game activities that reinforce the Bible lesson

- Closing, worship, music praise time, skits, mission project reminder, outreach, encouragement

- Organize a family night for the evening of the final day or the next Sunday so that the parents are able to see what the children have been learning all week. This provides an opportunity for the parents and family to be in the church building to receive a warm welcome from congregational members and become comfortable with the facility.

- Provide publicity for church, Sunday School, and future children's ministry events.

- Offer the church Board of Evangelism or Outreach Board information on visitor families for follow-up and outreach.

Optional:

A Friends and Family Night Vacation Bible School, nighttime VBS, allows for more volunteers and for people of all ages to attend. Dinner can be served before the VBS begins. Offer babysitting for babies and toddlers, and add groups for children, teens, and adults to gather for VBS-themed Bible classes. Everyone can gather together and be included in the openings and closings each night.

The Board of Children's Ministry
Charter

(Church name)

Membership

The Board of Children's Ministry (BCM) is led by the chairperson and made up of the Sunday School Head Coordinator, Cradle Coordinator, Department Coordinator, Children's Music Coordinator, Children's Fellowship Coordinator, Children's In-Reach/Outreach Coordinator, the Director of Children's Ministry (as ex officio), other special coordinators assigned, and any other interested congregational member age 18 or older who is a voting member of the church with a heart and passion for children and their faith development. Terms begin (list when here) of each year.

Meetings

A chairperson is appointed at the first meeting of each year. The chairperson will call meetings, coordinate time and place, prepare an agenda, and conduct the meetings. The BCM will meet at least once quarterly, more if needed. Annually, someone from the board will be appointed as secretary and prepare minutes for the other BCM members and the church council. The BCM will submit a written report of the activities, accomplishments, and budget needs to the church council no later than the end of September of each year.

Goal

Children's ministry is implemented and maintained at (name of church).

Purpose

To meet the needs of the children's ministry for the spiritual good of the children, to help parents fulfill God's command to teach their children about Him (Deuteronomy 6:4–9; Ephesians 6:1–4), to recognize the child's example of faith (Mark 10:15), and to give children opportunities to express it (Matthew 18:1–5; 21:16).

Objective

The BCM will work together in harmony to communicate, discuss, coordinate, support, and encourage the children's ministry.

Activities

- Encourage each other and pray together with any requests to include God's continued guidance in plans, decisions, praises, and thanksgivings for the children's ministry.

- Evaluate existing and propose new programs, classes, and events in accordance with the goals of children's ministry.

- Along with the Director of Children's Ministry (DCM), create job/ministry descriptions, and continue to change and/or update, when needed, the Children's Ministry Blueprints.

- Coordinators report and share information.

- Discuss possible solutions to concerns, problems, and special situations, and rejoice in accomplishments and successes.

- Support and help with decisions proposed.

- Responsible, along with the DCM, the Sunday School Head Coordinator, and the Sunday School Teachers, for special worship services (Christmas, etc.) and Sunday School events.

- Support, pray for, and encourage the DCM in activities, programs, and events.

- Assist the DCM in obtaining new coordinators, directors, and any other volunteers when needed.

- Assist the hiring board of the congregation in obtaining a new DCM and child-care attendants when vacancies occur.

Reflection

How is the children's ministry developing? What progress has been made? Are the goals being reached? Is this board working with other boards and committees when necessary to fulfill the mission and vision of the congregation?

*Please note that not all church bodies write a charter as a part of their constitution. Others write bylaws or use another structure. When preparing an official/legal document, such as a church constitution, using the correct words and grammar for clarity is very important. What is written in the church constitution is like a "solid." It can only change with a congregational vote. So, keep it brief, keep it simple, and include important policies that rarely change. Blueprints for Children's Ministry are like a "liquid." They can change frequently as the needs arise. Whenever possible, try to use leadership and team-work-type words instead of management words. Follow Jesus' example!

Sample of events to invite other boards to help when needed:

Fellowship Board

- Rally day/Sunday School & Bible class picnic
- Fall Harvest Fellowship
- Hearts for Jesus Valentine's Day activities
- VBS family fun night

Board of Christian Service/Human Needs Board

- Hearts for Jesus mission project
- Providing for member families in need

Stewardship Board

- Distribution of children's offering envelopes
- Educational newsletter articles about children's giving opportunities
- Placing recycle bins

Trustees Board

- Painting halls and classrooms
- Hanging pictures and bulletin boards
- Windows in classrooms

- Air circulation/cooling/heating
- Fire escape/emergency plans in each classroom

Outreach Board/Evangelism Board

- Kids' Night Out—Bible Blast!
- New Life Festival
- Vacation Bible School
- Sunday School publicity in the community

Worship Board

- Acolytes
- Christian education Sunday/rally day
- Family Christmas worship service
- VBS closing worship service

I Can't Wait to Be There!

KEB

Kim E. Bestian

Notes

Notes

Notes

Notes

Notes

Notes

Notes